Borders, Human Itineraries, and All Our Relation

THE ALCHEMY LECTURE

Borders, Human Itineraries, and All Our Relation

DELE ADEYEMO

NATALIE DIAZ

NADIA YALA KISUKIDI

RINALDO WALCOTT

Introduction by

CHRISTINA SHARPE

Duke University Press Durham and London 2024

Published by Duke University Press, 2024
Published by arrangement with Alfred A. Knopf Canada,
a division of Penguin Random House Canada Limited
Printed in the United States of America on acid-free paper ∞
Designed by Jennifer Griffiths
Jacket design: Jennifer Griffiths

Library of Congress Cataloging-in-Publication Data
Names: Adeyemo, Dele, author. | Diaz, Natalie, author. |
Kisukidi, Nadia Yala, author. | Walcott, Rinaldo, [date] author. |
Sharpe, Christina Elizabeth, writer of introduction.
Title: Borders, human itineraries, and all our relation /
Dele Adeyemo, Natalie Diaz, Nadia Yala Kisukidi, Rinaldo Walcott ;
introduction by Christina Sharpe.
Description: Durham : Duke University Press, 2024. | "Published by
arrangement with Alfred A. Knopf Canada, a division of Penguin Random
House Canada Limited". | Includes bibliographical references.
Identifiers: LCCN 2023046771 (print)
LCCN 2023046772 (ebook)
ISBN 9781478030775 (paperback)
ISBN 9781478026532 (hardcover)
ISBN 9781478059769 (ebook)
Subjects: LCSH: Boundaries (Philosophy) | Identity
(Philosophical concept) | Decolonization. | Ethnicity.
Classification: LCC BD.B68 2024 (print) |
LCC BD392 (ebook) | DDC 111—c23/eng/20231108
LC record available at https://lccn.loc.gov/2023046771
LC ebook record available at https://lccn.loc.gov/2023046772

CONTENTS

INTRODUCTION

In times like ours, times of great crises—climate catastrophe, human catastrophe, ecofascism, all kinds of fascism, authoritarianism, the complete breakdown of so-called liberal democracies, and more—great thinkers/writers/makers and organizers across fields, disciplines, and geographies are thinking about, and moving on, bringing another world into view. They are imagining from and into the possibilities of living in other ways. And they are thinking together, sometimes in public, about the times we live in, the legacies of anticolonial struggle, the futures of the planet, the textures and futures of precarious life.

The first Alchemy Lecture happened live in Toronto in November 2022. We cannot help but notice that this coincided with the timing of the 27th UN conference on climate in Egypt, where the deep hypocrisies of those who hasten the catastrophe with rapacious extraction were on display—even as the movement of people fleeing climate and economic degradation is called "an invasion," even as people are threatened with deportation, and even as they are condemned to situations made unlivable by these capital practices. There is much work to be done—and there is much work *being* done—to make the relations, human and more than human, in which we might be able to really live. Each of this year's Alchemy lecturers knows this—molecularly.

We could not imagine a more engaged and urgent set of thinkers and makers to address this year's theme: "Borders, Human Itineraries, and All Our Relation." They are all public intellectuals, writers who are deeply engaged in their time and world; and as polymaths, they all work across genre. Their thinking is a source of newness, of brilliance, and of deep engagements.

We did not want intellectuals who spoke from the position of defending or ameliorating the status quo. Rather, we invited these four thinkers because, as their work and practices make clear, they know that this current world is made from the catastrophes of colonialism and genocide and slavery. These intellectuals were formed in the crucible of *that* brutal worlding, and they also know that there is another way, that there are multiple other ways—other means by which we might approach or encounter the world.

What resonates most profoundly from the words of architect, artist, and critical urban theorist **Dele Adeyemo** (UK/Nigeria) is his attention to Black infrastructures. He is telling us that "*Wey dey move* calls forth the way we must all learn to move, on increasingly uncertain and shifting grounds."

And he offers this coruscating sentence: "They dared to block their infrastructure for profit with the infrastructure for another world."

———

The poet **Natalie Diaz** (US/Mojave/Akimel O'otham) tells us that "like story, migration is a sensual movement of knowledge. . . . Both story and migration are an alchemy. They catalyze change and transformation." And she asks us, "What is the language we need to live right now?" And, "Where is the future located?"

Language, she asserts, is for living in—it is constitutive of how we imagine and structure past, present, and future relation. She says, "Our relationality has to exist outside Settler State borders of meaning. We require a language beyond the English language of citizenship. I don't seek our future *We* and *Us* or dream our relational practices from inside the vocabulary of the English language. Like Sixo, in Toni Morrison's *Beloved*, like our ancestors before us, I don't believe there is a future seeded in the English language."

Philosopher **Nadia Yala Kisukidi** (France) writes us into a poetics of Diaspora. She asks: How to tell the story of this spatial concatenation of diaspora? What is its language? What type of writing does it require us into? Seeking an answer, she arrives at the marvelous, saying: "Such is the purview of the marvelous: narrate life, in its insolence, and fly in the face of negation."

And then she offers this: "For diasporic lives, when we refuse to consider them as ambassadors or figures of national loyalty or betrayal, repopulate the world with wonderful fables"—ones that tell the continuous stubbornness, in other lands, in other countries, of men and women who walked barefoot, making the places of human future more fertile.

———

Cultural theorist **Rinaldo Walcott** (Canada/US) asks us to consider inheritances in excess of white supremacist logics—an "inheritance of feeling, which is something more than a feeling." He tells us: "Invention, then, is our inheritance too."

He goes on to say: "Present migrations, and coming migrations produced in the vortex of climate catastrophe—which is to say produced in the context of the last five-hundred-plus years—makes thinking about borders more urgent." And, "Climate change and climate unpredictability, and the migrations that flow from these, will have people moving to where the resources for living a life are being hoarded. They will be moving . . . towards the resources that have been extracted from their lands and turned into all manner of consumable and financialized products of our late-modern lives. At the heart of present and coming migrations lies a reckoning with global theft, the maldistribution of the earth's resources."

He leaves us with a question around and from which to imagine all our relation: "What might it mean to live a life, if we can't risk desiring and working towards utopia?"

As those of us who were present at the live lecture thrillingly witnessed in November 2022—and as all of us can see in the pages that follow—by asking these questions, and by creating these conversations between and among disciplines and geographies, these four vital contemporary thinkers have come together and created alchemy.

—CHRISTINA SHARPE, Toronto, 2023

RINALDO WALCOTT

Invention, then, is our inheritance too.

What environments must we foster to
imagine the world anew after the undoing?

DELE ADEYEMO

Wey Dey Move

The Black Infrastructural Life of Sedimentary Circulations

DELE ADEYEMO

ONE. Door

In the beginning, the world was created by the spreading of sands over the primeval waters. Olodumare, the supreme being, the Alashe—the generator of Ashe, the vital power that enables the sun to shine, the moon and stars to glitter, the winds to blow, the rain to fall, and the rivers to flow— gave Oduduwa a sacred bird and a bag of sand, instructing him to descend from the sky to transform the liquid world into habitable land.

Oduduwa poured the sediments onto the primal waters and placed the sacred bird, a guinea fowl, upon them. The bird, a special giant creature, used its huge claws to dig and spread out the sand, creating dry land where there was once water. Where the claws dug deep, valleys were formed; and in the space between its scouring talons, hills, uplands, and mountains were left. The place where Oduduwa accomplished this task was named Ilé-Ifẹ̀, the place where the earth spreads.[1]

How is it that the design of a doorway can undo the world? I'm moved by this question, which haunts Dionne Brand's poetic exploration in *A Map to the Door of No Return*. If, as myth tells us, the world came into being by the divinely ordained circulation of sediments, the fact that the door's construction might be eclipsed by the spiritual and psychic rending it created, rippling through space and time, underscores architecture's ability to shape ontology.

Brand explains that "the Door of No Return is of course no place at all but a metaphor for place. . . . [It is] no one place but a collection of places. Landfalls in Africa, where a castle was built, a house for slaves, *une maison des esclaves*. Rude enough to disappear or elaborate and vain enough to survive after centuries. A place where a certain set of transactions occurred, perhaps the most important of them being the transference of selves."[2]

As a collection of places, the door is an infrastructural component of what Alexander Weheliye would call a "racializing assemblage," one that derives its meaning as an extension of the slave ship, the Middle Passage, and the plantation, lashing together periphery and metropole through the modern legal and financial instruments of credit, property rights, and insurance—a global infrastructure of innovations that legalize theft, underwrite abduction, and monetize rape, murder, and genocide.

I'm interested in the spatial dimensions of processes that hold our lives in relation. How do the environments that surround us condition the possibility of our being? What is the shape of sociality, and what are the architectures of relationality?

The door is such an architecture that has molded the conditions of possibility, creating a rupture in all directions, drawing ever more souls into the catastrophe that radiates from its site. As the persons abducted into slavery across the

African continent were funneled into the singularity of the doorway, West Africa was pulled across a threshold—with catastrophic consequences as the chaos of slave raids and tribal war was loosed upon the continent. Centuries of internal conflict alongside the imperial expansion of African states created economies dependent on sending captives into the slave trade. African kingdoms, and the fabric of society within them, began to crumble as leaders turned inward, on their own subjects, to maintain the supply of human flesh. Whole villages and towns were emptied out and people lived in terror.[3] In a terrible irony, the most advanced and organized African societies became the biggest suppliers of slaves.[4]

Radiating out from the focal points of coastal slave factories, colonial infrastructures accelerated the extraction of wealth, creating the conditions for colonial circuits and forming new patterns of urbanization.[5] The global circulations foundational to modernity were, in other words, only made possible through the complete fragmentation of African society. The switch from the slave trade to colonial administration signaled a transformation in capitalism, a transformation calculated to effectively dominate the flow of materials and labor. As Du Bois argued, in Africa abolition was an instrument of colonization, and British rule was in fact strengthened by the antislavery crusade as new territory was annexed and controlled under the aegis of emancipation.[6] When immediate colonial rule became too expensive, decolonization according to neocolonial logics was instigated.[7] By the time slavery was abolished, the door had ushered in increasingly expansive infrastructures for the continued extraction of Africa's wealth.

Even today, as the door decays to ruins and dust, its presence continues to structure the flesh and blood, the soil and the liquid geographies left in its wake. And behind the Door of No Return, inside the oldest of all the slave factories, we find yet another door: a trap door leading directly from the female's dungeon to the governor's bedroom. Like the Door of No Return, and the bloodstained gate of Frederick Douglass's narrative, the trap door is evidence of the construction of a billion primal thresholds that, if we dare to peer through, reveal the monstrous intimacies in the making of the infrastructural subject.[8]

Infrastructures extend the doorway, regulating existence, enabling or restricting movement, marking the bodies that traverse their thresholds. As defined by anthropologist Brian Larkin, they are "built networks that facilitate the flow of goods, people, or ideas and allow for their exchange over space . . . They comprise the architecture for circulation, literally providing the undergirding of modern societies . . . generating the ambient environment of everyday life."[9] In short: "Infrastructures are matter that enable the movement of other matter. Their particular ontology lies in the fact that they are things and also the relation between things."[10]

Our lives are splintered, enclosed, tethered, and circulated by these infrastructures of modernity.

Crucially, infrastructures are not inert. As Graham and McFarlane highlight, infrastructure is "not just a 'thing,' a 'system,' or an 'output,' but a complex social and technological process that enables—or disables—particular kinds of action . . ."[11] Infrastructures are therefore heterogeneous assemblages of lively processes involving technical and natural, human and other-than-human agents—all of which constitute infrastructural lives. Yet, to fix our gaze on those monstrous portals of the slave factory brings our attention to the fact that certain lives that constituted its infrastructure had to be unthought.[12]

Just as the Middle Passage could not erase the consciousness of a culture as splendid and ancient as the classic cultures of traditional West Africa in the new world,[13] neither could the extractive infrastructures of modernity on the continent. Entangled within the infrastructural lives of the slave factory were forms of consciousness that took shape in environments outside the limits of its control.

When the newly created land below the sky was ready for occupation, the supreme being commissioned the creativity deity, Obatala, to mold the first human images from clay. The images were then infused with Ase, or individual souls, and placed inside the lower, female half of the cosmic calabash—in the manifestation of the womb—so as to be delivered by pregnant women.

Humanity, eniyan, was charged with the responsibility of transforming the primeval wilderness below the sky into an orderly estate. Ilé-Ifẹ became a great settlement from which civilization spread. And the philosophy of its people, known as Ifa, traveled across the world.

The creation of the body by Obatala is commemorated in the name "Oosasona," meaning the deity created a work of art. It signifies that the body is a divine artwork that makes the soul manifest in the physical world, thereby defining individual existence; and artistic creativity among humans as a spiritual act, and a material expression of Iwa, the character of the soul.[14]

If, in Yoruba mythology, the fashioning of the world represented an understanding of beings' inseparability from our embodied relations to each other and the earth, what environments must we foster to imagine the world anew after the undoing? What new relations come to light if we think through how myths, personal histories, and everyday lives become entangled within and through infrastructural life?

I can't say exactly when I started this work. Perhaps it was sometime soon after I began my PhD, when, in the course of conducting my research, I realized that my life history provided an intimate knowledge of the postcolonial upheavals of the Structural Adjustment Programs (SAP) inflicted on Nigeria, having been born into that crisis at the moment the country's economy went into free fall.

Or perhaps it was during the slow-burning awakening that followed the first wave of the Black Lives Matter movement, when as a young aspiring architect I realized that despite the assumed neutrality of my education, I could never be just a regular architect. I felt the impossibility of practice dawn as my awareness gradually grew that architecture was a racializing instrument of urban development, unevenly shaping the patterns of daily life.

I'd like to think that the story begins much earlier, though, with my naming. As is the tradition of the Yoruba, my paternal grandparents named me. In their eternal wisdom they chose to call me Olubamidele—"God has guided my path home"—despite the fact that my parents settled in Nigeria several years before my birth. How could they have known, then, that I would only spend the first five years of my life in this country, that I would leave and lose sight of this place, only to return in adulthood? The meaning of this proverb that was my name only fully resonated with me many years later, as an adult, and several years after the passing of my grandparents, when I found myself traveling for the first time in Nigeria without my parents, having grown up and lived most of my life in Scotland. African names are often projections of the parents' or guardian's wishes onto the infant, and Yoruba names are typically phrases that communicate something important about desires for the life of the child and the world they are born into. And yet I had never asked what the intentions were surrounding my naming, or given it much thought, until this visit.

Perhaps it was when I was in the back of a taxi telling the driver my name. "Ah ah! Oyinbo! So you are a Nigerian? Do you know what your name means?" Yes, I said confidently. I had been telling people my whole life the literal translation—but in this moment I suddenly realized what it meant to me. Until now I hadn't considered the possibility of my return, as my name foretold, not just as a visitor but as a part of this world. I felt my grandparents speaking to me through these words with a foresight that even they had been unable to articulate in our many conversations when living. The moment hit with an overwhelming rush of warmth and gratitude. Silence fell over me as the bustling streetscape scrolled passed my window, and I slumped in my seat, with revelations of my name's meanings continuing to unfold. "I am here, I am home in a place that until now I could only imagine as a distant destination." So it was that my inheritance began to reveal itself at the moment in my life when I was ready to understand. And wrapped within these realizations was an even deeper meaning that revealed itself. Perhaps the journey home is an ever-unfinished story? Even when a semblance of home is found, it remains dependent on fragile relations that must be continually maintained.

It occurred to me that by the time of my birth in Nigeria, my grandparents had already lived in the UK, started careers there, then returned to Nigeria: a journey of homemaking from a village near Ibadan to London and back, connected by a string of accumulated friendships and extended family. I decided that, as part of my conscious journey toward home, I would make a pilgrimage to the beginning of the world. Traveling against the grain of underlying migratory trends, I took a shared taxi, a regular four-door sedan, where I was crammed in with three other strangers and their belongings as we drove along the Lagos–Ibadan Expressway. I would stay in Ibadan, the ancestral home of my grandfather, for several days with family before journeying to Ilé-Ifẹ̀, the ancestral home of the Yoruba.

More than sixty years before, moving in the opposite direction, my grandparents would have taken a more circuitous route from Ibadan to Lagos, along a road twisting through my grandmother's ancestral hometown of Abeokuta. Like many others migrating from rural settings before independence, they traveled in a repurposed British military transport. Sitting on fold-down wooden boards, my grandmother with her three young children on a days-long journey rocked back and forth along winding roads following my grandfather, who had traveled a year ahead to London. In this new world created by the colonial order, the only route to continue his development was to study for a degree in the UK. From Christian primary school to Anglican grammar school, and then to missionary college in Sierra Leone, he had followed the path for bright students cunningly designed by the British through religion and education to further the colonial worldview. The allure of university led to the reality of him and my grandmother traveling with their young family as part of the first wave of the "Windrush generation" that were drawn into the infrastructural life of empire to help plug the postwar labor shortage in Britain.

The journey from hinterland to coast was simplified with the opening of the Lagos–Ibadan Expressway in 1978, in the last days of the short-lived military government of Olusegun Obasanjo, which lasted for three years, from 1976 to 1979. It was the first rural expressway in Nigeria, cutting 127 kilometers through deep mangrove rain forest, laying gravel sediments and concrete to connect the former capital of Nigeria with the capital of Oyo State. And when it was opened, commuters were mandated to pay a toll to cover part of the expense of its construction.[15]

Now, so many years later, the expressway was in a terrible state of repair, with crater-sized potholes large enough to destroy a car's suspension. Our driver, like those of other vehicles on the road, had a reckless belief in his abilities, swerving in and out of traffic and around obstacles with unrelenting speed. For the past twenty years, German contractors Julius

Berger have been dragging out the reconstruction of the road, often causing large sections of one half of the dual carriageway to be closed.[16] When this happens, commuters find themselves using the same narrow road as oncoming traffic, each stream driving with the same cavalier spirit despite the lack of a central barrier. What should be a simple hour-long journey often becomes an exhausting trip lasting several hours as the construction, traffic, and accidents form go-slows. This creates the opportunity for mobile markets of street hawkers to appear, squeezing in between the still cars, selling every imaginable fast-moving consumer good—but these are no less dangerous than the road itself when bandits take advantage, robbing commuters trapped in static traffic. As we speed along in the taxi, passing piles of sediment and concrete from never-ending roadworks and the burnt-out shells of oil tankers and car wrecks from previous accidents, it feels as if we're playing an all too high-stakes game of chicken in which no one is prepared to give an inch.

Traveling along this road, which carries 250,000 commuters daily, whilst contemplating its history, my grandparents' journey punctuates to me how, as we go about our lives, we are captive to infrastructures that are continually shaping the directions in which we move. When these infrastructures fail, the lives they maintain and the hidden assemblages that maintain them come into view, revealing the sets of relations that they structure from the social to the political-economic scale. As I experienced the discomfort of traveling the road, the Lagos–Ibadan Expressway revealed to me how the lives of its commuters make up the raw material for a wider systematic program of exploiting infrastructural development for the enrichment of elites and Western consultants. Constructed during a critical moment in the modernization of Nigeria, the highway marks a transition in the exploitation of infrastructural life. No longer just a tool in the extraction of raw material commodities, with the construction of the road, through the structure of its contracts, infrastructural development itself had become the mechanism through which value is extracted from everyday life, with devastating consequences.

TWO. The unthought

Passing through the Door of No Return meant reentering the world as the infrastructure of that infrastructure. It meant being transmuted into a fleshly component of the infrastructural assemblage of racial capitalism.

How, then, should we regard the position of this hidden, unthought life that undergirds infrastructural lives? How do we account for the absented presence, or the forgotten spaces of forgotten space?[17]

How might we come to value those who were, as Harney and Moten describe, "not just labor but commodity, not just in production but in circulation, not just in circulation but in distribution as property, not just property but property that reproduced and realized itself"?[18] This is, as Tiffany Lethabo King writes, "Blackness as . . . raw dimensionality (symbol, matter, kinetic energy) used to make space."[19] An existence in contingent relation to the world, with no ending or beginning, and "the standpoint of no standpoint, everywhere and nowhere, of never and to come, of thing and nothing."[20] Black infrastructural life describes the forever-resource mined by recursive cycles of extraction.

When I arrived in Ilé-Ifẹ̀, I was excited to have finally reached the place where, it is told, the world began, and eager to learn what I could about Yoruba philosophy in this ancient holy city. And I was thankful to be hosted by friends of a friend. Damilola and Kayode were a married couple who happened to be my age mates, working as academics teaching history in the University of Ifẹ̀ while running side hustles as they raised their three young children. Their commitment was inspiring. Whilst diligently performing the role of loving mother herself, Damilola was doing impressive research into archives that reveal the British colonial government's efforts to reconstruct Nigerian motherhood through infant welfare services.[21] Whilst in their home it struck me that we were all around the same age my parents had been when my family had left this place—which made me ponder how different things might have been had we stayed.

When the country began to slide into the condition that Wole Soyinka would call "the Open Sore of a Continent," with military coups, mass unemployment, and hyperinflation, my parents tried to hold on as long as possible, letting go of luxuries and prized possessions first, then the basic essentials, until the moment arrived when all we had left was just enough to get out or be forever trapped. Meanwhile, my hosts Damilola and Kayode had, as children, lived through martial law, food rationing, kill-and-go police squads, and the menace of armed robbery, with no possible escape. Almost overnight a viable industrializing economy with a currency close to parity with the dollar was plunged into a crisis from which it has never recovered, taking with it the emergent middle-class and bringing a new wave of chaos and insecurity.[22]

As a petro-state, Nigeria had greatly benefited from the OPEC oil embargo and the energy crises of the seventies that caused the price of crude oil to escalate. Nigeria's exports became dominated by oil as rapid industrialization ensued. The expansion of federal government spending on transport infrastructures, public housing, manufacturing, and other state enterprises was achieved at the cost of neglecting the traditional export crops such as peanuts, cotton, cocoa, and palm products.[23] A great flow of rural dwellers into the cities and larger urban centers unfolded, necessitating the import of basic commodities such as rice and cassava to feed a more densely concentrated population no longer living from the land. In a move to capitalize on the migration to urban areas from what seemed like every village in Nigeria by siphoning off vast amounts of public money, politicians devised a populist, nationwide federal housing project for low-income earners.[24] The demand for construction cement exceeded the capacity of domestic production and imports skyrocketed, hemorrhaging the nation's foreign exchange reserves and making a market for the importation of sediments. The creation of the supply chain was so sudden and opportunistic that an armada of vessels laden with cement extended so far out from Lagos harbor that it reached into international waters.[25] Even with the cronyism and profiteering, when oil prices were peaking and revenues increasing, unlimited development seemed possible. But with the end of the fuel crisis in the late 1970s, the country found itself caught in a trap, unable to service its debt burdens. Overnight, a nation's citizens were rendered once more as the unthought lives of infrastructure—their existence transmuted into the guarantors of an intergenerational debt.

Before my hosts take me to see the historic city of Ilé-Ifẹ̀, Kayode gives me a tour of the university. And as we sit in a shaded *buka* on the edge of an empty staff car park, eating a lunch of some of the best *amala* I have ever tasted, like childhood friends reunited, Kayode tells me with an infectious enthusiasm about the life that he had experienced but I had left. During the tough times in school, to make light of things, he and his classmates would play a game where they would describe in code which meal in the day they would have to skip. "I was a zero-one-one, some others would do one-zero-one." If things were really hard, he might say, "Zero-zero-one." As long as he had something to eat before bed, he said, he was okay.

The leafy campus of the University of Ifẹ̀, was one of those now-creaking state institutions created during the time of rising optimism in post-independence Nigeria. During the oil boom of the 1970s, it had been designated a federal university by the military government and became an impressive institution of knowledge production. The writer Wole Soyinka had lived and worked there, and during the slide he had personally witnessed the impact of the kill-and-go squads.[26]

We visit the university bookstore and I pick up a book on Yoruba proverbs and Soyinka's play *Death and the King's Horseman*, first performed at the University of Ifẹ̀. At first read I struggle to follow the complexity of traditional cultural life it paints through its sophisticated use of Yoruba proverbs.

It's in the history department, when I learn about the research of Professor Akiwowo, that I find the key to understanding the Yoruba origin myth in relation to the philosophies I will hear about in the ancient city.[27]

In the center of Ilé-Ifẹ̀, I was surprised to find a modern urban landscape that, at first glance, betrayed few traces of its antiquity. But as I was guided around the center of Ilé-Ifẹ̀, commonly known as the City of 201 Gods, visiting some of the numerous shrines and meeting with the elders, I began to realize that the history was contained in the language and cultural practices, and forms of sociality shaped by the architectures of the city's emergence. Yoruba folklore tells us that humanity was created here in Ilé-Ifẹ̀ and the region was one of the earliest organized settlements in the tropical forests of West Africa. Surrounded by hills that formed a natural high bowl at the confluence of many streams flowing through the undulating landscape, a collection of settlements began to form—a network of small, autonomous kinship groups, *elu*, with their own hierarchies of chiefs, each creating a world centered on its own shrine and rituals.[28] From this region Yoruba societies spread hundreds of kilometers across the tropical forests in an area now defined as southwestern Nigeria and reaching as far as modern-day Togo and Benin. For at least fifteen centuries, most Yoruba people lived in *elu* settings, the structures of which remain ever present in the culture of the Yoruba—in the composition of their towns and cities, in the structure of their communities and chieftaincy institutions, and in their religious, economic, and social institutions.[29]

Archaeological records suggest that settlement groups existed from at least as early as the fourth century BCE,[30] and by the eleventh century CE, Ilé-Ifẹ̀ had emerged as an important city-state producing sophisticated art. It often goes understated that long before the famous Benin Bronzes came the more lifelike terracotta and bronze sculptures of Ilé-Ifẹ̀. But as trade shifted toward the Atlantic coast with the arrival of the Europeans, the city diminished in importance, surpassed by the kingdoms of Oyo and Benin. Nevertheless, it remained an important spiritual center throughout British colonial rule. Indeed, the British policy of *indirect* colonial rule meant that, in principle, traditional structures were left in place to control their local populations: two worlds running parallel. In reality, the everyday traditional institutions of the regional kings and chiefs were entered into the infrastructure of empire forming what Peter Ekeh has termed as 'two publics' where the moral order of Indigenous society was splintered by the introduction of Westernized civil structures.[31] We see the impact of this condition play out in *Death and the King's Horseman*, where, despite the two systems, the British intervene, with the aid of Westernized natives, in the ritual suicide of an esteemed (yet corruptible) elder whose duty it is to follow the king in death as his horseman, so that his soul may be accompanied in the afterlife.[32]

The story reveals the catastrophe that befalls Indigenous society with the imposition of a so-called "civilizing colonialism" where the moral premise of the preservation of life is the cipher for intervention, inflicting a form of epistemic violence which threatens once more to undo the world.

In fact, the preservation of life particularly through the management of tropical diseases across Africa had been a vector for creeping colonial governmentality.[33] As the colonial order spread deeper into Yorubaland through such strategies, more and more people were drawn in greater numbers from rural and inland settlements like Ilé-Ifẹ̀ toward the epicenters of the colonial administration, in urban areas and the increasingly regulated coastal threshold of Lagos harbor. The closer people traveled to the coastline, the more they found their myths and social architectures disrupted by colonialism's spatial imaginary. In Lagos, where malaria was the greatest cause of mortality and the principal barrier to colonization, the British mosquito control program extended beyond the typical sanitation plans of segregating colonial accommodation from Indigenous populations through *cordons sanitaires* to encompass dredging and swamp reclamation. This in turn caused the deforestation of mangroves as displaced Indigenous communities sought new means of income and sustenance.[34] The imposition of the "colonial civilizing" project therefore resurfaced in the reshaping of the watery landscape surrounding Lagos through anthropogenic circulations of sediments.

Lagos was originally a collection of small islands within a lagoon system occupied for hundreds of years prior to colonization. The site did not emerge as an important trading point in slavery and the Atlantic trade until the late eighteenth century. Rising from a Benin war camp in the sixteenth century to become a major Atlantic slave port in the 1790s due to its strategically central position at the intersection of a lagoon network that spanned the Bight of Benin, the city was an important independent city-state in local trade.[35] When slavery was abolished in all British territories in 1833, merchants flouted Britain's naval blockade and the city's Obas continued in the slave trade. Finally, in 1862, King Dosunmu, the Oba of

Lagos, ceded the city to Queen Victoria as a British "colonial possession" after several territorial configurations that followed the demolition of the city by British naval bombardment in support of British antislavery measures.[36] When, in 1914, Lagos was made the capital of the amalgamated protectorate of Nigeria, the British constructed an artificial channel across the sandbar where the mouth of Lagos Lagoon opens to the ocean. The seawalls erected to allow ocean ships access into a section of the lagoon waterways at Apapa, where the colonial port was developed, would forever alter the natural flow of errant sands that circulated along the coastline. And wherever urban expansion took place, it developed along the axis of colonial infrastructure extending out from the seaport and reaching almost a thousand kilometers inland, along a railway line built to transport raw materials from the interior to the coast.

Since the annexation of Lagos, development has therefore been characterized by the forced dispossession of Indigenous communities, expropriations of land by state and private enterprise, the dredging and sand filling of natural swamps and mangrove habitats, and the expansion of port infrastructures. Yet communities whose forms of sociality are centered in Indigenous practices have persisted. Simultaneous to colonial developments, Indigenous settlements formed adjacent to colonial infrastructures and in lagoon-side locations by people migrating from inland settlements. Planned independently of colonial infrastructures, these Indigenous settlements and lagoon-side communities are therefore repositories for traditional belief systems and other ways of being that have gradually become engulfed by the modern city.

About eighty years before my grandparents made their way from Ibadan to Lagos en route to London, it had already become common practice for places like Ilé-Ifẹ̀ to encourage some of their citizens to migrate to the bigger cities. As the now late Oba Bashiru Oloruntoyin Saliu of Oworonshoki explains: "I am a descendant of the founder of Oworonshoki who came from Ilé-Ifẹ̀ and settled in the place called Oworonshoki today. He came with his crown from Ifẹ̀ and that is the same crown I am wearing today . . . At that time, there were many shrines that were brought from Ilé-Ifẹ̀ to Oworonshoki."[37] The Oba recounts how the lagoon-side community of Oworonshoki began to thrive after the Ifa oracle was consulted; it gave instruction that a sacrifice must be carried out to prepare for the coming of people from places like Delta, Edo, Benin, Niger, and Ogun (Ijebu), among other riverine areas, to trade in the community.[38] As the colonial port developed in Lagos, Indigenous communities were sent there from inland settlements like Ilé-Ifẹ̀ to establish trading posts. When they traveled, as had been practiced since the emergence of the social structure of the *elu* that developed from the Ifẹ̀ bowl, the people took their shrines and their ritual practices with them. And as one of the masquerade acolytes in Oworonshoki explains, every couple of years there would be a great masquerade celebration to welcome newcomers into the society.[39] Oworonshoki, like other lagoon-side communities in Lagos, was therefore the result of an Indigenous form of planning that reaches back into the mythical origins of the Yoruba people. And it is often here in places steeped in mysticism like Oworonshoki that the children of the parents and grandparents who traveled away from their traditional settlements as rural life was transformed meet with fresh waves of migrants to the city.

THREE. Sediments

Through my film project *Wey Dey Move*, which was exhibited at Het Nieuwe Instituut in Rotterdam and cowritten with my long-term collaborators Hermes Chibueze Iyele and Sunday (Valu) Obiajulu, I trace the entangled relations among the sedimentary circulations on Lagos Lagoon, revealing the absented infrastructural lives that shape the megacity's infrastructures as they are articulated in the wake of slavery and colonialism.

Lagos is a megacity of 24 million people, with an estimated two thousand migrating there daily from across West Africa. The legacies of slavery and colonialism have set in motion a great migration, one that is accelerating as the infrastructures of extraction—from the slave factory to the mega-port—intensify development along the coastline, drawing more and more people across the threshold of no return.

The rapid expansion of Lagos provides an example of the roles that sand and sediments play in constructing our infrastructures. It highlights what the writer Amitav Ghosh calls the "great derangement" of a global trend that intensifies colonial patterns of urbanization through continued development on coastlines, even as they are eroded by climate change.[40] After water, sand is the world's most consumed natural resource. And as the urban planning scholar Nehal El-Hadi declares: sand builds our worlds, and yet our demand for it is destroying the world.[41] Its apparent abundance is abstracted from the unthought crisis of its extraction. This process repeated all over the city is most spectacularly exemplified by the private development of Eko Atlantic City—a billion-dollar luxury real estate development that reclaims over ten square kilometers of land from the ocean. Built where the now-legendary Bar Beach evaporated into the sea, the waterfront used to be one of the very few public spaces in the sprawling city. Providing a natural civic space, it has now been eroded by the depleting presence of the colonial port.[42] And so the beach that was cut off from the nourishing flow of a river of sand that circulates in the Bight of Benin as part of nature's littoral drift is now substituted by private developments. Through the changing sedimentary circulations, colonial infrastructures resonate, continuing to compound catastrophe upon catastrophe.

In Lagos, as this pattern of urban expansion unfolds, shorelines disappear, riverbeds are devoured, and ecosystems are destroyed, all in the voracious consumption and circulation of alluvial sediments.

On any given night, well after sunset, when the day's heat begins to radiate from the ground, a fleet of sand divers sets sail from Sandbeach in the community of Oworonshoki on Lagos Lagoon.

In the black of night, thirty to forty vessels, each operated by a crew of two or three men, are carried by a light breeze and subtle currents. These boats use a combination of the technology of the traditional West African canoe, which is piloted using a long pole, and the European sail and rudder rig. Allowing themselves to drift, these crews float on the waters of the lagoon until they arrive at a shallow-lying sandy shoal, close enough to the surface for a diver to reach on a single breath. Here, they will drop anchor and rest for the night with their boats braced together. The men huddle under their sails as blankets.

At dawn, these crews will begin diving for sand, descending up to four meters below the surface whilst using rusty metal buckets to gather the sediments. They dive naked to avoid the weight of wet clothes, plunging over and over with little pause for rest, until their flat-bottomed barge is so laden with sand that the gunwales barely reach above the waterline.

This is risky, arduous work. Collecting sand from the sea-bed stirs up clouds of sediments that hide threats such as large fish with razor-sharp teeth, poison jellyfish, and flotsam from marine wreckages.

Braving these dangers, the divers make up to fifteen dollars a day—or more if the wind allows a second trip. In Lagos, sand is categorized and regulated as a mineral, making these men subaquatic miners. Yet there is no protective union or industry regulation, and so the divers are self-employed laborers who cover all their own overheads. By relying on the wind, and using sails made from sewn-together rice sacks, the sand divers reduce their energy consumption and costs.

Commercial sand dredgers follow the divers like vultures, scavenging the most easily accessed sedimentary deposits for their machines to suck and pump the sand back to shore. This is a process that the anthropologist Anna Tsing describes as "salvage capitalism"—one where wealth is extracted from natural and human processes occurring outside the conditions that capitalism controls.[43]

As the fleet of sand divers returns to shore, the sails on the horizon echo the ghosts of the much larger galleons that loomed over the Atlantic coastline for more than four hundred years, spiriting away those who would soon become the unthought life that was central to the infrastructure of an emergent global capitalism. When Europe's ships came to compete for slaves, ivory, and gold, amongst their trading cargo of manufactured goods, firearms, textiles, and alcohol was a sedimentary load: Portuguese, Dutch, Brandenburger, and Danish bricks transported as ballast. Parapets, quoining, vaults, and underground cisterns formed the infrastructural components used to rapidly construct the factory central to slavery's circulations ahead of the Middle Passage.[44] By the time the ships departed, the weight of these infrastructural sediments had been substituted for the weight of the bodies that they were shifted and shaped to contain.

In Ghana—in famous places like Elmina and Cape Coast, and in forgotten locations such as Butre, Princes Town, and Komenda—the ruins of the infrastructure of the slave factory can still be found.[45] But the material catastrophe they created weighs heavier than their presence. For every boatload of bricks, how many boats loaded with souls were transported? And even in the low-lying lagoon geography of Lagos, where defensive forts could not be built, the slave ship became the factory.

Today, as the divers' sailing boats return to the shore laden with a cargo of fine alluvial sands that pour into the lagoon from the ocean and via multiple tributaries, the pattern of foreign infrastructural development repeats. Once the sand reaches the shore, the load enters the market as filling sand for land reclamation, or to be combined with cement to form cinder blocks and concrete for the city's expanding settlements. The industrial output of European dredgers such as Van Oord, Royal HaskoningDHV, and DEME dwarfs the production of the artisanal miners as, once more, sediments circulate for the construction of extractive infrastructures—ones that are predicated no longer on the export of commodities but on the extraction of value from everyday life.

More than just the hidden labor of capital, the sedimentary circulations of the lagoon reveal the entangled forms of unthought life that underpin infrastructural development. Sedimentary extraction repeats the exploitation of Black infrastructural lives—the series of hidden, multi-scalar assemblages of everyday social, ecological, and climatic lifeworlds upon which infrastructural processes have always depended.

FOUR. Lifeworlds

Lagos Lagoon is the product of thousands of years of shifting sedimentation. As riptides move thousands of tons of sand, depositing it in temporary banks, the eroding process of tides forms gullies, creating deeper depressions and more powerful waves. Sandbanks accumulate silt and debris. Mangroves and other vegetation begin to grow through this natural process of land formation.[46] Through the action of heavy surf and the continuous longshore drift, the shoreline is molded into a sandbar—separate from the ocean, a liminal space emerges as a shallow body of water in the form of a shoal.

The lagoon as a shoal, as Lethabo King highlights, is a geological formation that compels our awareness of our contingent relation to nature. Like Black thought, it is "a place where momentum and velocity as normal vectors are impeded. It is a place where adjustment needs to be made . . . the shoal requires new footing, chords of embodied rhythms, and new conceptual tools to navigate its terrain."[47]

The lifeworlds of the lagoon are therefore repositories of other ways of being precisely because they result from migrations and patterns of movement that return our focus to the mythical story of the beginning of the world—and its description of the relationship between the primal waters and shifting sediments. How, then, might the lagoon's hidden lifeworlds, with the mysticism, ecologies, and social histories that constitute what I'm calling Black infrastructural life, open up the possibility for new assemblages and conceptions of the human?

It is the morning after the night before—the last day of Slum Party, a festival organized by my collaborator Valu and his team, held at the place they call "Power Base" in lower Oworonshoki. Last night I finished my filming well after dark, just in time to catch an Uber back to my uncle's house in Surulere. The event was bigger and busier than I'd ever seen before, and the partying will have carried on till late.

I arrive shortly after dawn. Valu has arranged for me to travel in Mr. Koja's canoe so as to record him fishing using the traditional method of the Akaja, a technique employed throughout the Bight of Benin, which uses cut mangroves to create large fish traps in the middle of the lagoon. Mrs. Koja, who has practically adopted me while I've been filming, as usual feeds me freshly fried young tilapia and *garri* mixed with water and sugar, teaching me phrases in Yoruba, and laughing at my pronunciation. When I fell sick a little while ago, I learned the importance of the mangrove not just for fishing and firewood but as medicine: Mrs. Koja made me *Agbo*, a special antimalarial remedy concocted from the aerial roots of red mangrove trees, boiled together with local herbs. Earthy and bitter, it is miraculously effective in settling a stomach or arresting a fever. The British could have avoided so much dredging and sand-filling in the fight against malaria, if only they could have trusted the prophylactic powers of *Agbo*.

As Mr. Koja's daughters, Tope, Koyin, and Janet, tell me that their daddy is originally from the Republic of Benin he interrupts them to staunchly insist he is a Nigerian. Although his parents arrived in Lagos from Benin, Mr. Koja has been fishing these waters for over sixty years, and he tells me there isn't a single spot on the 6,500 square kilometers of lagoon that he doesn't know how to fish.

Jumie, who is Valu's chief assistant for Slum Party, as well as being the children's dance group organizer and leader of the mothers' exercise club, is on hand to translate. Because Jumie is coming along on today's trip, Mr. Koja's daughters Koyin and Janet want to come too. And because they are bored and can no longer sleep, Valu's assistants Wisdom and Isaac also decide to tag along. Before I know it, these two are lugging a huge boom box into the fishing boat.

As we leave our corner of Oworonshoki, the Afrobeat of Adindu Victor's track "Confession" kicks in:

My darleeen, would you fly with me, inta-nash-an-al
You go dey with me for flight[48]

I realize that we've entered an unmarked watery highway. Our boat taxis along an invisible track, our perspective of the shore revealing not a slum but a series of villages on the lagoon, slowly awakening to the day.

It's the beginning of harmattan season, when for three months the trade winds blow desert sands from the Sahara over the city. In the coastal location of Lagos, harmattan is not as dramatic as in the Sahel, but the light, dusty fog that fills the sky this morning is enough to dim the sun, drying out the atmosphere, providing a break from the relentless humidity while subtly dehydrating mouths, scratching at throats and nostrils, and turning knees and elbows ashy gray.

As we leave Oworonshoki behind, the rest of the city melts into the distance, and the lagoon begins to shift our consciousness. We accelerate into a mercurial silver expanse that disappears into the horizon. Lagoon and sky merge. An atmospheric haze surrounds us and thoughts drift. We are moving north, away from the more choppy lagoon waters that exchange with the ocean. Stretching before us like a great, quietly murmuring intelligence is an impossibly still, boundless liquid plain. In this moment, the entangled relations of the spiritual, ecological, and social clarify and, slowly, the lifeworlds of the lagoon reveal themselves.

As Lethabo King describes, the shoal is a space that is simultaneously land and sea, one that fractures established identities of Blackness, showing them to be overdetermined by watery metaphors of rootlessness; and also fractures identities of Indigeneity, showing them to be overdetermined by fixed imaginaries of land as territory.[49] The entanglements of the infrastructural life of lagoon dwellers encompass both Blackness and Indigeneity foregrounding how these subjectivities are able to simultaneously navigate the nature and urban space. In so doing, I would argue, the unthought assemblages of their lifeworlds open a portal into how we might imagine the world otherwise, through a "radical reconstruction and decolonization of what it means to be human."[50]

As I picture them, the assemblages of Black infrastructural life encompass radically open-ended relations alongside indeterminate conceptions of the human—ones where the more-than-human, in the form of ancestors and spiritual possession, and the other-than-human, in the form of natural processes in nature, coexist. More than the flesh and greater than a single being, the assemblages of Black infrastructural life reveal what it means to consent to exist in relation—a notion captured in the Yoruba philosophy of *Asuwada eniyan*, which as the late Professor Akinsola Akiwowo explains, the ability of humans to form purposeful bonds to live together as one entity.[51]

FIVE. Refusals

Linking us to an ontological totality, the assemblages of Black infrastructural life can be found everywhere in the life-sustaining spaces formed in the face of unbearable odds.[52] Black infrastructural life is in the everyday fugitive acts of the undercommons, and the beautiful experiments of wayward lives.

It's in the places that nurture freedom dreams and the diasporic infrapolitics of resistance.[53]

It's in the sonic geographies of care.[54]

It's in the Black Chapel, and the carnival and the masquerade.

It's in the secret garden plots of slaves on the plantation.

It's in the intimate relation to nature maintained by Indigenous peoples.

It's in the whispers of rebellion carried on the wind.[55]

It's in the market women's protests.[56]

It's in the slum—anywhere you find a DJ and a sound system and bodies letting rip, dancing with the youthful, frenetic energy that comes with living life on the edge of catastrophe. Rhythmic, virtuosic outbursts of accumulated tension that help to, as the Oworo-based artist Wayde raps, *"make I dey far away from sapa... make I no be friend to suffer."*[57] With limbs charged with the spirits of their ancestors, the children of Obatala invent the future, creating new movements, queer movements, satirical movements, political movements, and loving movements, in an infrastructural web of care.

Here in the "Trenches," as Saidiya Hartman describes it, is "an urban commons where the poor assemble, improvise the forms of life, experiment with freedom, and refuse the menial existence scripted for them."[58] As a settlement conceived of in the world where the spirits live, the terrible beauty of the slum is that it never really was a slum, but an infrastructural assemblage of another order.

The Black infrastructural life of existence in the "Trenches" not only describes the people as infrastructure[59] but also the ways in which its assemblages of agents and bodies exceed that infrastructure. The way that they/we/dey[60] move is always already greater than the self. As a social body emanating from uninhabitable spaces, in rhythms of endurance on demonic grounds,[61] it was these spaces that formed the movements that carried young people into the streets protesting against corruption and police brutality. When the global wave of the

Black Lives Matter protests sparked by the public murder of George Floyd at the hands of Minneapolis police on May 25, 2020, opened a portal to connect Black diasporic struggles, it was in these spaces that the protests of Nigerian youths, both in that country and across the world, gained momentum.

It was in these spaces—after the lockdowns that starved more than they saved, and after the brutality, intimidation, and extrajudicial killings perpetrated by the arm of Nigerian law enforcement known as the Special Anti-Robbery Squads (SARS) were piled on top of all the intergenerational indignities of living lives in the wake—where youthful protesters gathered at Lekki Tollgate, and their energy shook the Nigerian establishment to its core.

And when the demands and spirit of the protests expanded to become a wider refusal of the corruption that had put SARS in place, threatening to undermine the structure of transnational debt obligations that enriches Western institutions and a comprador elite, the movement could no longer be tolerated.[62]

In the face of such a dynamic coalition of local and diasporic actors calling for change, an element of Nigeria's ruling class calculated that extreme measures were necessary to stop the movement in its tracks. At the Lekki Tollgate on October 20, 2020, at least twelve people were killed when officers of the Nigerian Army opened fire on a peaceful protest, quelling the #EndSars movement.[63] A subsequent independent judicial investigation concluded that "the manner of assault and killing could in context be described as a massacre."[64] But the state's recourse to this spectacular violence—a violence so shameless and callous as to recall the actions of bygone

military regimes—only highlighted the fact that a new antag-
onistic consciousness has awakened: a precarious urban
youth whose vital infrastructural power can no longer be
hidden from them.

"I no dey move dat way. Don't make me move dat way . . ."[65]
sang Reekado Banks to commemorate the peaceful protesters who were shot to death by the government, tearing open
on "Ozumba Mbadiwe," yet another primal threshold like the
Door of No Return, because they chose to barricade the main
highway into the city. Because they dared to block that infrastructure for profit with the infrastructure for another world.

WEY! . . . Wey dey move! W-e-y, d-e-y, m-o-v-e is a Nigerian
pidgin term meaning things change and constantly evolve. It
underscores the way communities have learned to move
through improvised, anticipatory, and provisional relations
that underpin the assemblages of hidden infrastructural lives.

And if the door, the expressway, and the tollgate appear
as hegemonic thresholds of power, funneling our existence
into reservoirs of private wealth, then their edifices collapse
when we consider the hidden intergenerational lifeworlds
upon which they rest, because these infrastructures are
haunted by the infrastructural lives that make them.

Wey dey move describes what it is to be a body in constant
motion consciously moving, traversing, and troubling thresholds as we carry within us the knowledge to imagine other
worlds. *Wey dey move* calls forth the way we must all learn to
move, on increasingly uncertain and shifting grounds.

DELE ADEYEMO

What environments must we foster to imagine
the world anew after the undoing?

What is the language we need to live right now?

NATALIE DIAZ

Fusings

NATALIE DIAZ

Alchemical Dream of We

Here, I won't speak in metaphor. Let me speak in memory, and in remembering, let me return to our bodies as having been dreamed, and as having been the dreamers. Let me say, *We* and *Us*, and let it be a divine occurrence, not *on* land but *of* land, having happened and having yet to happen, in transformation and arrival.

The mountain dreamed me and I dreamed the mountain—a flesh-being bearing its first dreamself. I dream the stone I am of and the stones I am among. *'Avii Imaanvenych*, we say—*We are of the mountain.*

Of as reciprocity. *Of* as a responsibility to tend and be tended. *Of* as toward the world, a practice of living, for and with others, not alone but among. Autonomous lives in collective living.

Since water is the first body, we are also *of* the water. *'Aha Makav*, we say, because the river happens to our bodies as it happens to our lands. Cut a channel into my chest and the red water will rise up and overrun it, a rivering. The river from which I came. The river *of* which I continue to become. I carry it in all my bodies—flesh, land, dream, beloved. I am *of* the water's abundant eruptions and dangerous satiations. From the river I learn the course and currents of love, of the living-ness that emerges from love—how to witness and wash, how to jump and break, when to soften or carve, sink or carry, when to hold or tread or dive, babble or flood, to shape while being shaped, how to drink, how to thirst, how to clean what is in me but not of me.

I have abandoned the metaphor, so I can hold the river. Not in my hands or my mouth. Not in my bowl or my cup. I hold the river in my body and in this holding I behold my being and its relationship with our world.

I am in alchemy with the river. In the water, I learn both what I am *of* and what I become. A fusing—to return to our first body of water and to the knowledge system of our original liquid form. This knowledge shapes a methodology of cycle, how to be among the earth and the sky, the plants and ani-mals, how to move with, against, toward, and through one another and our worlds—in rush, flow, and current; in hold or carry; crystallizing; vaporing; cleaning; ebb and tide; reorgan-izing gravity and pressure; to fall; to still; to recharge.

If this fusing is our call to acknowledge our body of water, a way to recognize our bodies as connected to one another, let us say, *There are only two directions—to be turned toward the water or to be turned away from the water.* We are of con-sequence to one another—the river, its body, your body and mine. How we embrace the world and enact our desires upon it through our practices of thirst and quench, desire and sate, determines the world we live in and how we know it anew, as a relative.

As it is with our waters, let me say, *I am of consequence to your body.*

As it is with our waters, let me say, *I am a consequence of your body*.

We live within the consequences of a relational *all*. *Mat tayuuch*, we say, from the verb *ataay*, which is the way the *all*, the *We*, the *Us*, happens. The *all* is our occurrence in this world. We who are the imagining of both land and water, thus created in their image from their elemental desires. We are the body of land and the body of water become other bodies. Nitrogen, carbon, iron. Clay and oxygen. Hydrogen, salt, and bone.

We are the flesh-manifestation of land's and water's dream. In this reciprocal dream, we must also do the dreaming, from within the created world toward the world we must help create. The alchemical *We*. Transmuting, passing, crossing, in migration and language toward and away from one another, carrying and carried by our stories.

The Rock Who Cried

When the Creator died, the story of his death trembled the valley, carried by wind and light, by the Colorado River, which we call 'Aha Haviily. Word tumbled along the river's bed, in ripples and waves that jumped the banks. The story echoed the rushes of rivercane, who quavered and snapped under the weight of the loss. The loss was carried by the clouds who, heavy and tired with this original hurt, fell in long shadows that slipped down the sand dunes. It moved in thunder along the riverine cliffs where the grieved swallows busted apart their mud homes and rent the water's surface, gnashing at the mosquitoes and flies swimming there. In one of these ways or another, the mountains and rocks learned of the Creator's death. One small mountain, small enough that it was mostly thought of as a rock and not a mountain, was overcome by the news and dropped to the ground and wept. The rock's grief was old and it cried for its whole life, for the life of the Creator, and for all its relatives the Creator had given to life. The rock cried and cried and cried; as it did, its color deepened and darkened. It cried in such a way that even today it stands out purple-red along the beige-blue ridgeline, as if it is still wet and weeping. As if it is still struck with grief, as if it is both hearing and carrying the story of the Creator's death. 'Avii Himiich is its name, or The Rock Who Cried.

The Rock Who Cried is not myth or metaphor or anecdote. This is a story of one practice of migration. Like story, migration is a sensual movement of knowledge, a system of how one receives knowledge and how knowledge arrives—the same way we arrive to and receive of one another. Both story and migration are an alchemy. They catalyze change and transformation. Migration reminds the flesh-body that it is *of*—of the river and the mountain, one story among many stories of living, one grief among many griefs, an energy that is not the beginning or the end but a process out of time. To migrate is to risk that this world can change. To migrate is to risk that our lives are of consequence to the world that has yet to occur.

The Circle as Surround

As Mojaves migrated across the desert and along the rivers, toward the Gulf of Mexico and Pacific Ocean and then back from those waters, they marked stories on rocks where they stopped for rest or shelter. One of the stories or symbols left for others was a dot with a circle drawn around it, sometimes called a circumpunct. Those small marks were messages to who might come behind them, and possibly to remind themselves of this text, if they arrived to that place again. The dot with a circle around it can generally mean, *Don't pass here.* More precisely and generously, a dot with a circle around it, *There are other ways to pass beyond this one way.* The circle surrounding the dot is a resounding, an image calling us to imagine outward, beyond the singular or particular way of seeing and knowing, moving through or across. An invitation to strike and reverb, to be of consequence to a collective movement.

This is land knowledge, which doesn't mean we know something about the land, rather it means we are learning to live in the ways land lives. Not just the marking on the stone conveys a language. The language itself is the practice of possibility-making in the surround and resound of the land— the single line of the circle amplifies the myriad pathways yet unknown, and the choices we might make as we share and fuse new and old traditions of arriving and receiving one another in land and water. These knowledges were taught to people by the land, as part of its relation to us, its tending and weeding, its seeding and harvest of us.

Not all knowledge is for everyone, but such land and water knowledge as this one is legible to and used by those who are willing to defy the map and look into the surround. The surround is where relation occurs. As the word *relation* suggests, this is the knowledge for those *called back* to the land and water before colonial surveys and properties.

Where am I if not in surround of you, my strangers and my beloveds? How often is the dot of my life, the way I choose to mark or don't realize I am marking the world, ungenerous to everyone but me? How malleable or porous must I be or can I be to those moving with me or against me, toward me or away from me?

The dot surrounded by a circle does not mean I can't pass or cross here—rather, it is a warning and a wondering, about what will be asked of me if I decide the pathway I am on is the only pathway, or the easy route. It is a message about what moving in the way I am moving will require of my body, of my life, of those I love and those I don't yet love, who are in migration with me, seen or unseen, known or unknown, here or in other lands and waters, whom I need and rely on to see me in their surround.

Mat Tayuuch

One way I try to understand the concepts and practices of relationality is through the language we use to express it. I begin thinking about most complex concepts through etymology. I chase the written word back as far as I can, migrating through its many origins and textual episodes—its early dreams, its optimisms and plans for progress, its terrible acts, its beloveds and its enemies. I read the story the word's ancestors told— the moments when its people transformed themselves for better or worse and thus changed a word's intention or memory, thus changed or at least masked their own intentions and memories. Then I set that English word alongside my Mojave language in order to find the English word's limits of imagination and generosity; places I might pressure or tweak its memory; how I might reorganize it or demand a greater capacity for our lives within its meanings or understandings.

I set the word *relation* next to the Mojave phrase *mat tayuuch*, which I invoked earlier. *Ataay* is an unknown, an unquantifiable and therefore ever-possible, ever-capacious *all*. It is the *all* that must remain undefined and yet held, carried and storied, like water, like river—it must be ready to be more abundant, more inclusive, more of itself, until its *We*, its *Us* is gathered and fed, convened and armed, corrected and returned to the fold, dreamed so they can dream. *Mat tayuuch* is a practice that refers to both land and body, an act of *relating* people and land to one another in a great constellated story. In these tellings, all things Mojave, all things imbued with life force, were touched and held, in name and in narrative, of where they'd been and what they had done, and how we were *of* and in relation to those stories. No architecture, or roof, or room can hold *mat tayuuch*. There could never be enough windows to open. It was first spoken outside where the stars showed its infiniteness. It often took numerous people to tell, and it stretched beyond any historical records of time or map, beyond any colonial order of temporal or spatial relationships. There is no line long enough. The lands and waters spoken of in *mat tayuuch* have Mojave names. The people also have Mojave names, and it was they who dreamed our first dreams. In the knowledge system of *mat tayuuch*, where the *all* is an action, a way of land and people occurring, I learned that my life is only as possible as the lives around me and that my actions and inactions are of consequence to and a consequence of the *all* I am *of.*

What Is the Language We Need to Live?

When I wake up in the morning, I ask myself: *Natalie, what is the language you need to live right now?* I mean the language of words, speech and text. What should we talk about when so many words exist to destroy us? How to speak the language made of words that deny us, and realize us in capture, humiliation, wound, or murder?

The border. The patrol. The wall. The bullet. The ballot. The line. The State. The State Park. The Nation. The spaceship. The oil. The man camp. The pipeline. The pipe. The copper. The mine. Theirs. The dam. The museum. The Church. The priest. The high-capacity magazine. The semi-automatic. The repeating firearm. How it repeats. The Occupiers. Their Occupation. Their religion. Their map. The property. The work. The wage. The water. The policeman. The body cam. The white man. The white woman. Their children. Those citizens. Those individuals and their freedoms. The task force. The unmasked. The brotherhood. The money. The sugar. The taxes. The membership fees. The self-driving cars. The recalls. The apologies. Their medicine. Their opioids. Not my brother's opioids. The warrant. The sentence. The inside. The outside. The university. The End of the Pandemic. The Blood Quantum. The Pledge of Allegiance. The law. The court. The concertina wire. The cyclone fence. The visiting

hours. The trade agreement. The desalination plant. The
grid. The chicken. The eggs. The layaway. The committee.
The other committee. The faculty. The monocrop. The crop
duster. Wheat. The microplasts. The rent. The landlord. The
president. The president's kids. The rising sea. The Territorial
Sea. The carbon. The BIA. The DOI. The DOAs. The detention center. The hidden detention center. The surveillance
tower. The satellite. The shipping container. The Prevention
Through Deterrence. The cages. The icebox. The Credible
Fear. The Settlement. The Settlers. The Settlers. The Settlers.

How might we speak of life beyond the State's designs and
borders? How to imagine the living we've yet to do if the State
language we have now is rooted in our suffering? What is the
language we need to live right now? Like the circle surrounding the dot marked on the rock by my ancestors, relationality
blooms in the surround and reverb of what was understood
and what was meant. It is rooted in that unknown space where
we are illegible and irreconcilable to one another, in the lush
spaces between and among us, where we are not touching and
are not known.

To relate is to not know, and it is to be alongside in that
unknowing, which is not an undangerous relationship. For
example, the snake doesn't know me with her eyes—I don't
reiterate what she knows when she sees me. The snake arrives
at me by tasting the air surrounding me, licks together the
atmosphere that holds me. For the snake, I am also what I am
not, and we meet in that condition, in the way I move through
the world and reshape the atomic. The snake gathers my
chemical reaction to the world with her tongue, pulls it in
behind her fangs, and lifts my scent into the Jacob's organ

located on the roof of her mouth, where those chemicals become who I might be in any direction of her. For the snake, I am a sensual alchemy of enemy, beloved, predator, prey, and wonder. The body language of our bodies in relation exists outside the typical definitions by which life is measured.

I'm not suggesting we need the snake languages my relatives have spoken. English is the context for my Settler State, and it also violently contextualizes my beloveds beneath its lexical infrastructures. Our relationality has to exist outside Settler State borders of meaning. We require a language beyond the English language of citizenship. I don't seek our future *We* and *Us* or dream our relational practices from inside the vocabulary of the English language. Like Sixo, in Toni Morrison's *Beloved*, like our ancestors before us, I don't believe there is a future seeded in the English language.

Sixo calls us toward a different listening, a practice of tuning in to our *before language* and *after language*. Despite the hundred years war English waged to silence my Indigenous language, it has been taught to me. My Elders outlasted our nations' lexical designs to destroy us. I have my language to speak about love, a love I deserve and a love I am capable of. I have my language to speak about dreams, through which I learn of our existence before English and through which I will imagine our existence after English. For Morrison's Sixo *then*, and now for me and for *Us*—this *other language*, this *before language* and *after language*, is a choice we can still make.

English has always frayed beneath our presence inside it. Our Native and Indigenous languages, our ways of water, our stories, our griefs, our *allness, ataayk*—for which English has such small capability—bear again and again on it. We tremble it. We falter and doubt it. There is no English language without *Us*, and while I am often in it or beneath it, I am not of it or its values. It isn't going to teach us how to speak to one another about the world we are dreaming.

I don't believe English was seeded with our future, but I am also *of* the desert. I have witnessed the bright-green desire of the mesquite tree to grow from darks seeds tightly sheathed in its golden pods. And how the land, water, and animals collaborate in the marvelous labor of scarification to ensure the seeds break free and take root. In flash floods, the slick brown seeds are beat against stones as they are rocked over and through the washes, hammered against hard surfaces, which break the seeds from their casings, spreading them across the sands where they will grow. When the flood has yet to come, the Coyote, our teacher, feasts on the sweet pods, eating them whole or in ragged chunks, shredding the husks, releasing the seeds into his belly and intestines. Then he wanders off into the desert, stopping here and there to shit out the seeds, where they will eventually sprout. Though there are other designs by which to create life and beauty, this relationship of *wantneeds* is an important story of the desert. English never believed itself to be a garden or field in which we might bloom, but we also learn from Coyote that we can grow and cultivate abundance from shit, even the shit of a Settler State.

June Jordan's "designs of revolution"

For the last several years, I have carried an image of a page from one of June Jordan's spiral notebooks. It was sent to me by the poet Solmaz Sharif, who took the photo on her phone and texted it to me while researching in the Jordan archives at Harvard. She sent it to me because Jordan studied architecture, and I have an obsession with furniture, in particular lamps and chairs. I am interested in the power that furniture and architecture have over our relationships and interactions with one another—how each can prophesy our bodies into action or inaction, into rest or restlessness. I am compelled by the ways furniture shapes our imaginations of one another, how it can control our bodies, urge us to touch, to look, to disengage, to dream even. The bedroom. The HUD house. The classroom. The courtroom. The museum. The library. The prison cell. We walk into a room and suddenly have an idea of what we deserve in an hour, in a conversation, in a meal, in a life.

In my Mojave language a chair is what you do. It is a place. That place is where the verb can happen. The chair came after our body and mimics our body. The chair becomes the impetus for the body to act even though the body was what the chair was shaped after. However, in the current hierarchy of furniture, if there were no chair, I might not sit, though the body can rest without the chair. For example, if I were to sit on the floor, in my language I would be doing the thing the chair is, *hinaak*. The chair is not a thing except in an architecture of power, except in asking or demanding the body to act, or not act.

The chair becomes the site of where the body can rest and therefore its presence determines its possibility. I can offer you my chair, or I can pull the chair out from under you. I can throw the chair in the funeral pyre when you die, so you have a place to rest in the next world. Or, more sinister, since the chair is firmly rooted in the power of furniture, the chair is also central to the design of many forms of punishment—to be forced to sit in a chair, tied to it, or to be denied a chair to sit in. The chair is designed to create a relationship between us and to define our future within that space.

In the image of the page I carry from her notebook, Jordan has written these questions, among others, in blue ink: *How to design tables and chairs for a really new life? Will we still use knives?* I interpret her question, at least partly, as implication that it is the "civility" of the table that requires we make and use knives. The more advanced the civility or civilization, the larger the table required to seat equally large men around, where they prophesy more terrible knives and more sinister meats to turn them upon.

The chair exists as a place for a thing we must do and only becomes itself when we do that thing. How many national historical paintings and photographs exist of kings' tables; and around which how many wars were drawn and signed into being; and what feasts were those men fed to fuel their long hours of war-making whilst sitting at those tables and chairs, with their big knives and pens, slicing away at the lands and waters mapped before them as if the map was our flesh?

Back to Jordan's questions: *How to design tables and chairs for a really new life?* The furniture she was referring to in the notes was part of her vision for "These designs of Revolution." She writes:

> *These designs of Revolution*
> *require a turning away from*
> *the enemy,*

They require a kind of going
up into the hills or
mountains, as did Castro,
scheming, around the clock,
a really different universe, or, as did Elijah, tuning
in-to a really different frequency
—the still small voice.

The still small voice recalls an old sensuality, one that is both illegible to the State's surveillance and also capable of speaking beyond it. The still small voice—of 'Avii Himiich, of Sixo, and of Jordan. The still small voice of the snake and her ancestral way of recognizing who I am of and how I am *of* her world. What is the "really different frequency" we need to remember or discover in order to be in best relation to one another, so that we might relate to and tend the living world we live in and, in doing so, tend one another? What is this frequency that exists outside or beyond the English language and its measurements of time and map, border and surveillance, labor and death? Is it a rock marked by a dot surrounded by a circle, urging us toward the beyond and resound? Is it a cry? Is it a song? Is it the way we turn our heads or hands? Is it a furniture we need to reorganize the spaces where we both come together and live apart?

If we are creating the world we want to live in now, what can we salvage from history's furniture? What station should we tune in to? Or how high up on a mountaintop or deep into a cave must we go to hear or sense one another's desires to live? The still small voice, I believe, is my voice. It is the voice I will hear differently because I have turned away from the enemy and toward you, where I will hear your voice first, and in the same way the snake recognizes me, or similar to how I carry the river in me, I will recognize my own life in your desire to live.

Where Is the Future Located?

And if English has no future in it, then where is our future located? Where in our mouths and minds, where in the marks we make, where in our texts and drawings, in our books or dreams?

I talk about the future, rarely knowing where it is, still unsure of which borders and boundaries of today are present there. Which ruins of the nation, the State, or my people will remain in that new or old place. The Settler State weaves its ideas of future into us—its empire, in some ways, can only exist in that future, where it keeps its people precarious and urgent *now*, in an emergency only the State's future can solve. I catch myself some days existing only in that future, which doesn't have to be an inevitable blueprint.

What will we mistakenly recognize as future because it is already in the image of the future the Settler State has defined for us? When we seek possibility, when we seek *our* future, whose should it align with or be alongside? What language, what language of consequence, do we or will we need, when those processes and desires for life seem not to align? How will we comport ourselves, if we decenter our individual emergencies and crises, and consider the emergencies and crises of others, of other beings and their processes and desires for life? How can we hold ourselves and one another accountable to turn "away from the enemy," as Jordan wrote?

When we say a language has no future in it, there are still other bodies in and of language we can turn toward or back to, as we face the morning and remember the land is not human, and beneath our human catastrophes, beneath our beautiful or painful suffering and bearing, the land and the water are good. The land and the water are our *before language* and our future. There is a *We* and an *Us* who are there now.

ALCHEMY HORSE

American they said + + but *Horse* I dreamed
                                    , and *Horse* became

              ++   ++   ++
    + ++   +++   ++   ++   +++   ++   ++
          +   +++   +++   +

+ + + I was cleaved + from human-earth + + +
Redsap lymph calcium + + + Atlas and femur
        , A new Chaos—
+ come forth + through the world's foaming + crust
        + + then licked + into my roan skin

+ + + A flesh being bearing + its first dreamSelf + + +

I came to life + + how stars appear—
        , Of dust + +

collapsed + till struck

+   ++

+ ++   +   ++ to light + + +   +

+ ++ +   +   + + ++

      Dream-erupted—
, Gila Monsters + lavablack + +

          +++ Land +++ +++ +++
               , All its thunders + + +

     In this great magnetic field + +
I am a knowledge system + + +

My hair is a tangled Mojave Dictionary + + +
     , And my tongue + is a danger + +

I speak a darkwhip + into the haboob's goldthrob + + +

This valley's bright-weather is my ceremony + + +
, Flashflood + is my medicine—
     + + how I clean myself of Self

+ + + America + + Hoard of Property + is a debris
     + of my cells— limestone + + wound-porous +
sea-floor + + basalt + trilobite + camel bones +
     , glass and Blackmountain + + +

+
+ + + +
+ + + + + +

+ + + We professional mourners + +
            crying for our lives + and for hire + + +
From dark-colonies + in the caves behind our hearts
+ + we weep the sun to fall + and bats into the sky

+ + + We weep the saguaros to bloom + Eastward
+ and moonwhite + + soft-petaled wounds +
            circling their night-wrists and crowns + + +
                    Grief is our lush and luxury—

        , The strain + of anything + that grows
+ + + Sand rose + + iron wood + + smoke tree + + +
We tend dune-gardens + from Deadlands + +
            till the halite beds + + reap selenite thorns +
from the horned toads' backs + + +

+ + + In the a.m. heatwarp + vultures
+ ripple the violet skydome + + +
A swarm of bloodgloved-archivists + + +
            They sky-write   + +
+ + + + +   + + +   + +
        + + +   + + + directions—
            + + + +   + + + +
        + +   + +
+ +   + +

, To the museum , To the university
        , To the hospital + + +

In this Epoch of Citizenship +
I must arrive everywhere twice—
        , Occupied and Unceded + + +
One hand *The Comet* + +
the other hand + *Who Makes the Comet Come*
+ + + So call me *Lodestone* + or *Alone* + + +
        Whisper me +
                , *Secret Magnet* + + +

In pink twilight + + my love and I are effigies
        + + leaching salt +
through our terracotta hands + + +

My language clays + + and maps +
amaranth lather + along my thigh—a migration
        + of Exile—
, A self-determined Relocation of pleasure—
                , wantneed + + +

We are the origin + + oxygen + and always becoming
        + + + Bloodworms
+ from which new land might grow + + +
        , How we make soil + +
then mud where we laid + + +

Alchemy of our wet denim skinz + and gravity + + +

We pulse animal and sensual + + +
        Thundercats of love + greening the desert—
, Pale grasses + fruit in my breath
        + + grey-green along the belly of the nightbranch + + +

        We are + unacreable
+ + + We abrade + the transit + the survey
+ + hold tight and repeat ourselves +
        in crystal lattice + + +

Come morning + + + Come Mercurylight + + +
We are blessed and scattered + + +
Shards + of a horsehead + water jar—
        , Lonely for a body + + and aching +
for the cool taste + and shape the first water once took + + +

This Nation + is a white bright + magnesium
        + NDN burn + + +
I fume and illumine + in its quantum-arson—
        , Indian Iron Alchemy Horse + + +

+ + + My brothers are the Cold Killers + +
shovelers + of silver anthracite + +
        fuelgods + of the midnight train

+ boxcar + jumptrack + jolt-light
+ + + Vaporing + + nightsalt + to cloud—
        , Mustanging + + +

Every desert highway is sacred +
        and gas station pumps + break our hearts + + +
We have pedal bones + white doctors call coffin bones
+ + + That's why I'm always dying—

        + + +That's why—
, I'm always halfghost + + half-back + + half-dressed
+ as the war party who will return—
, With a full tank of gas + + +
        , And a stick of scalps + + +

Tonight the city + + is a tectonic bone radio—
        , Our ancestors are on every channel + + +

Scorpions whip and fluoresce + from the shadows of Settler houses
Green-eyed wolf spiders + emerge from their dens +
        to join the dark hunt + + +

The midnight train + monsoons + around the bend
+ + recognizes me + as a relation + and cries +
        Chuk+Shon   Chuk+Shon   Chuk+Shon

        + +   + +   + +   + +   + +   + +
        + +   + +   + +   + +   + +   + +
        + +   + +   + +   + +   + +   + +

+ + + We are each + the other's + passenger + + +

+ + + On the horizon + my warriors volcano + + +
       + + + I shatter cinders + from my hair
+ + I'll watch them eat the day-aliens with flame
       + + + American + NDN + horse pyre + + +

The Hohokam canals + crack awake + +
gush their ghostwaters + through the settlement streets + + +
       blister + and boneflower + + +

I war whoop out + into the empty + displaced hip +
of the Ghost-sea + + and the Ghost-sea +
       war-weeps back +
spiraling + the etched shells of my ears + + +

+ + + A + M + E + R + I + C + A—
, Haunted hotel + shiprock + rockwreck + ship of fools + + +
       , Little giant cemetery + of braids

+ +	+ +	+ +	+ +
x	x	x	x
+++	+++	+++	+++
x	x	x	x
+ +	+ +	+ +	+ +
+	+	+	+

+ + + Beloved Occupiers + + I am posting notice—
      , There is no more vacancy + + +

When this world has ended + I will carry my people + Home
+ + +

NATALIE DIAZ

What is the language we need to live right now?

When it comes to art and creation,
the idea of a common, shared perception
is inconceivable. The truth is always a question.

NADIA YALA KISUKIDI

Walking Barefoot

On the Marvelous in Literature, Black France, and Diaspora

NADIA YALA KISUKIDI

Literature at the center

In mid-September of 2022, flipping through a French news-paper called *La Croix,* I stumbled upon a fascinating column by the novelist Estelle-Sarah Bulle, "Une certaine parenté."[1] The story begins in a highly descriptive manner with an unremarkable episode of daily life at a contemporary art space in France, not far from Paris. It is a story of everyday racism in the workplace. No slurs. No blows. No outbursts. A spontaneous conversation between colleagues that reveals the persistence of a racial ignorance—an ambient "nanoracism"—that permeates the air we breathe. From this anecdote the column took a surprising turn to consider the literary enter-prise. Literature and race. Literature and racism. How are we to write about these matters? How can we tell the stories whose threads are intertwined in a tapestry of racial fabula-tion? As a conclusion of sorts, Estelle-Sarah Bulle leaves us with the following sentence, which I will take up as a starting point for our reflection here:

> When I think, for example, of the Caribbean population I come from, and of its extraordinary richness, I am gripped by an existential vertigo at the thought that the recent

origin of this population is a succession of rapes committed by masters on slaves. At times we need supernatural, perhaps even fantastic, tools to write about this.

The kinds of violence inflicted on Black bodies, under the plantation system, were such that they appear inconceivable within our collective consciousness of this world. This makes it impossible to compose a narrative in which reason, our normal perception of reality in three dimensions, might remain intact. The precise nature of our case leaves us no choice but to break with verisimilitude as a norm for the literary text. But might the same not hold for other life experiences that leave us beset by vertigo? Experiences of lives lived in the face of death, and of violence, but also of the systematic dismantling of times and places, of lands we find ourselves driven from but cannot bring ourselves to forget? For this is exactly what happens in lives lived in diaspora.

Defenses of verisimilitude in literary narrative tell us that literary narrative should possess logical coherence and credible appearance—we must be able to believe that what is shown has taken place, or could. A fictional narrative, in this view, should not cast doubt upon a commonly held and shared perception of the world. Everything in it should possess an appearance of truthfulness that does not contradict our physical, habitual perception of the real. Within such narratives, we must be able to find our bearings, to never get lost—as if the written work consisted of data collection, deriving its worth through a relationship to the sciences.

In a country like France, where the name of Descartes is often invoked as a national symbol[2] to reterritorialize the history of reason, enlightenment, and clear and distinct ideas[3] by placing them within the Republic's borders, imagination is too often regarded with a wariness that borders on outright distrust. Truncated, impoverished, and in constant collision with veracity and reality, the excesses of imagination are readily associated with childhood, and thus a symbol of weakness. In our case, this is primarily a childhood of the mind—a state of mind that confuses time and space, believes in ghosts, in magical phenomena whereby the dead remain alive, in the possibility of other worlds beyond our own, and in spaces where all matter is endowed with life so that a stone, a reef, a tree, or a house may become a story's protagonist. In order for literature to be taken seriously (and perhaps to be consumable), it must resist all infantile regression. Such a regression will only be tolerated when it tells us stories of an exotic elsewhere, making the imagination a faculty of faraway worlds, which the French language confines to the periphery. At the center, the duty of literature remains a duty of truth, far from the imagination's "languages in madness" (Mudimbe) and from its dangerous effects on reason. Often, this duty is self-reflexive: literature should speak only of itself, and continuously congratulate itself for its ability to be more real than reality itself and truer than truth. Universal.

But reality, as we know, is not cut from one cloth. When it comes to art and creation, the idea of a common, shared perception is inconceivable. The truth is always a question. With regards to the so-called center, what is left to be said? It is defeated, dismantled, besieged from all sides. Even in European capitals like Paris whose architecture, street names, and urban infrastructure still pay tribute to the bygone grandeur of empire, the idea of the center can be routed and smashed to the ground. Let us recall the analysis of Ngũgĩ wa Thiong'o in *Moving the Centre: The Struggle for Cultural Freedoms*:[4] against the hegemony of the center—of any center—our response must be to "decenter." Decentering is as much a political act as it is an aesthetic one in the literal sense: it is an act of *feeling*. Decentering challenges the perception of the world as only one entity, recognizing the plurality of places possessing, claiming, or elaborating political, aesthetic, even metaphysical instruments for their own self-determination.

The decentering we are speaking of even applies to the "center" itself, which, in turn, is no longer the center of anything. As the center is plagued by its own periphery, by its neighborhoods, by postcolonial hordes who exist in arrangements of time and space that alter geographies and heritages. The North is decentered from within by a heterogeneity—a South?—that has gripped it. We should not attempt to understand this decentering using the paranoid terms of conquest or invasion, but instead with the welcoming and now widely current language of hybridization, creolization, and *métissage*. In *Postcolonial Melancholia*,[5] Paul Gilroy describes this process of decentering, showing how cosmopolitanism manifests in Britain and its cities, including London—a demotic, popular cosmopolitanism that is reconfiguring a specific notion of British national identity based on racial and cultural homogeneity. At the heart of these decentering practices, literature is metamorphosing. The center becomes unhinged. The art of literature no longer means fixating on the question of verisimilitude, but rather being open to new possibilities. If we could venture a hypothesis, I would like to float an idea: the question of verisimilitude in literature belongs to a specific world where cartographies are sure of themselves. A world in which space is represented according to the Euclidean norm of our agreed-upon perception of two- and three-dimensional physical space. A world where the principle of identity is respected.

The question of maps and space grows more complex the moment we acknowledge the experiences of lives conceived from places that seem, based on a common perception, implausible—the experience of lives in diaspora. The experience of living in at least two places at once. Conjuring up narratives which intermingle, fabricating new territories. To confront "dreamed countries" and "real countries," as Édouard Glissant would say. To discover that, beneath feet, the very earth itself is being gobbled up by corporations and chipped away drilling, until it gives way. To marshal the names of places, assigned within borders recognized by international organizations, on lands over which no people are sovereign. How can the language of verisimilitude account for the thing it holds implausible, though that thing remains a shared human experience: the experience of ubiquity?

Diaspora

Before returning to literature, I would like to linger a moment on the experience of living in diaspora. I feel that *ubiquity*—the ability to be in multiple places at one time, a quality often associated with divine beings—best describes the experience of diasporic life.[6] With its long Jewish and biblical history,[7] the term *diaspora* characterizes the history of human groups, peoples and other communities, who have left behind their countries, often under duress, to live in dispersion. Diasporic peoples cultivate a transnational mode of existence while maintaining affective, symbolic, political, and/or cultural relationships with their community and their land. To conceive of diaspora is to imagine a unit—a people, a country— simultaneously diffracting and multiplying. In every one of its multiplications and every new reflection, the origin maps out the possibility that allows a narrative to continue—even if that origin has ceased to be anything substantial. Ubiquity is a concatenation of times and spaces.

Prior to the question of identity, which is all too often conflated with the question of diaspora, life in diaspora is the direct, intimate, and subjective experience of spatial multiplicity that is simultaneously experienced. In diaspora, the borders of nations and countries—be they dreamed or real, defunct or solidly enduring—are superimposed, drawn into tension, and effaced. In this spatial concatenation, the outlines of a map (expanse, location, configurations of meaning and neighborly relations) are never clear or transparent. For one, because in diasporic experience maps are not conceived in the manner of the European Renaissance explorers who sought to understand the *terra incognita*[8] of a World that was, for them, *new*. Diasporic maps are rarely drawn as "curiosities," and often bear witness to "emergencies."[9] At the outset of their book *Terra Forma*, Frédérique Aït-Touati, Alexandra Arènes, and Axelle Grégoire interrogate the new cartographic exploration they are engaging in, breaking with the work of cosmographers to "generate maps based on bodies, rather than on topography, frontiers, and territorial borders."[10] This implies a type of mapping that moves "from the horizon line to the thickness of the ground, from the global to the local."[11] This formulation is interesting; their work, enriched by a Latourian, contemporary ecological reflection, foregrounds the viewpoint of the living, who are possibly but not necessarily human, and belong to a network of relations. At no point does their world become an environment external to itself. Nevertheless, the spatial concatenation that is specific to human life in diaspora remains subject to the issue of borders and territorial limits, a constant locus of tension and nexus of understanding itinerancy and its political, social, economic, and cultural implications: administrative violence, the hostility or hospitality experienced in countries of departure or arrival, the act of switching from one language to another, and more.

To grasp the spatial entanglements of life in diaspora, we must look beyond a clear-cut dualism that simplistically opposes the local and the global. Diasporic life partakes at once of the horizon line and the thickness on the ground. A global crossing of territories and a singular way of inhabiting them, of exploring them locally. Movement and sedentariness. Distance and proximity. Thickness and horizon. Unity and multiplicity. Local and global. The value of the word *diaspora* lies in shining a light on "a concordance of opposites."[12] A type of concordance that undermines common sense and our collective understanding of the plausible, of verisimilitude, and of reality that governs by a set of immutable physical and natural laws. In diasporic life, one can be the same and the other simultaneously, inhabiting several spaces and histories (national, communal, personal, etc.) at once. Neither personal origin, nor heartbreak, nor the quest for self-knowledge will permit us to immediately grasp the meaning of diasporic *existing*. Rather, it lies in the impossibility of locating this existence on any map whose expanse, borders, and locations can be fixed once and for all. By thinking spatially, we can move beyond the idea that identity questions are the only baggage we can bring with us when we think about diaspora.

A cartography of diaspora that combines thickness and horizon lines is not necessarily encouraging; the movements it maps cannot guarantee freedom from constraint or conflict. Into the multiplicity of spaces dreamed and lived in diasporic life, we must add a politics—literally, geopolitics—of movements on earth which determines the kinds of the relations of domination or depredation that bodies will be confronted with when they cross a given border.

Who are the troublemakers?

In this first quarter of the twenty-first century, reactionary forces swept over contemporary France and other Western countries that redefine political space around a rigid and closed conception of national identity—wherein one nation appears as a subject in itself, possesses a "racial soul,"[13] and is protective of its borders. In the old European nation states, migratory movements from the Global South to Global North, set in motion by a capitalist globalization that has compounded debt and inequalities, has unleashed vehement reactions expressed in myriad ways. The COVID-19 pandemic that struck Europe in January 2020 concentrated and accelerated these reactionary tendencies. In France, the far-right party, Rassemblement national, long discredited by the racist and inflammatory language of its first president, now appears to be a credible party of power. With the creation of new extremist parties (such as Reconquête! in 2021), the political institutional landscape is now home to a growing assortment of nationalist organizations. In this context, Black, Arab, Muslim, and other racialized minorities are construed as a figure of "the enemy within." And after the series of murderous attacks perpetrated by Islamic State, this once fringe position can now be heard across the political spectrum, blurring the line between conservatives and "progressives" (as shown by the debates around the French "Republican Values" Law of August 24, 2021).[14] In the ongoing "culture wars," newer fields of study reshaping academic life (gender studies, postcolonial studies, the decolonial option, critical race theory, and others) are met with opprobrium in an attempt to defend an immutable canon. Under the guise of protecting scientific objectivity from a militant degradation of research, certain political agendas are deemed "anti-French." During the same period, France has been reconfiguring its soft power strategy in its former African colonies, where its presence has been strongly contested in nations such as Côte d'Ivoire, Mali, the Central African Republic, and Burkina Faso. This strategy also includes wide-ranging efforts to develop memory policies about France's colonial and post-colonial history.

In this political context that combines a rigid reaffirmation of national identity with the return of imperial repression, we see at least two very concrete usages of the word *diaspora* (or of its idea, i.e., configurations of its meaning) circulating in the French public sphere, specifically with reference to African and Afrodescendant diasporas, and more generically, to diasporas perceived as Black and originating from continental Africa. Unsurprisingly, the term *diaspora* is undermined by the nationalist camp. Sometimes linked to the administrative question of dual nationality, the idea of diaspora troubles what Stuart Hall termed the "fateful triangle" of race, ethnicity, and nation:[15] the person living in diaspora appears not only as a figure of national disloyalty but also as a threat to the physical, cultural, and moral integrity of the nation. To be French, in this view, means confining one's history and dreams within the borders of a single territory. Ubiquity is a violation of the principle of identity.[16]

After the November 13, 2015, attacks in and around Paris, for which Islamic State claimed responsibility, French President François Hollande tabled a bill that would strip French citizenship even from French-born dual citizens. Though dropped after deliberations in the National Assembly and Senate, this proposal from the governing left echoes ideological elements of France's far-right party, whose political program in 2012 called for the withdrawal of dual nationality "outside cases of dual nationality with another European Union country."[17] In this view, one cannot be at once French and non-European. One must choose.

What is singular, and a break from the past, is how the term *diaspora* has come to be valued in a manner uncharacteristic of a French state whose republican ideal of citizenship was constituted in opposition to any affirmation of difference, so as to guarantee equal political rights for all. Both diplomatic and commercial, this new valorization plays out against the backdrop of France's attempt to rebuild facets of its

African presence while confronting the opposition of civilian populations and competition from other great powers, such as China, Russia, India, and others, who are unburdened by a colonial or neo-colonial legacy (a liability) in the region. In this context, African diasporas that have settled on French soil are expressly called on to become ambassadors for France abroad, especially in Africa.[18] France's policies of soft power (or soft diplomacy) are being redeployed in Africa to contain other imperialist threats and restore a national image permanently tarnished by the system of networks and influence, known as *Françafrique*,[19] that perpetuated French power in decolonized Africa, and carried out harmful French diplomacy during the 1994 genocide against the Tutsis in Rwanda. From this perspective, the idea of diaspora does not trouble the issue of nationhood; it comes draped in the colors of the French flag and helps formulate an ambivalence toward an understanding of integration in which Black representatives of France, whether citizens or merely residents, enjoy the right to put their differences on display only when such differences can be monetized. This vision presupposes that there are *chosen (choisie) diasporas* that receive, as a reward for their integration in the host territory, a right to a very slight difference—that which allows them to represent France, to its maximum benefit, outside its borders. In opposition to these are the *recalcitrant diasporas*, which can be described in the terms of a speech on separatism delivered by the President of France on October 2, 2020, where he invokes "children of the Republic, sometimes from elsewhere, children or grandchildren of citizens with an immigrant background from Maghreb or sub-Saharan Africa, [who are reconsidering] their identity through post-colonial or anti-colonial discourse."[20] The implication is that this discourse carries within it the germ of separation.

Two conceptions of diaspora have emerged: the "chosen diaspora," as a figure of national loyalty, to which a right to the slightest difference is granted for the benefit of a center that operates with imperial reflexes, alongside diasporas perceived as figures of national disloyalty (the "recalcitrant diasporas" or dual citizens, which are not exclusively European), who are impossible to assimilate into the center and the nation. It appears that whichever meaning and use is assigned to it, the idea of diaspora entails a principle of deviating from national identities conceived as homogeneous. For a center, jealously protective of its national identity and borders, the political problem becomes the following: how to destroy or control this principle of divergence?

Yet in use, diaspora proves to be a slippery concept. It mobilizes a set of closed narratives that together undermine the very utopian potential (its principle of divergence) that one might otherwise ascribe to it. It operates in a closed register that does not challenge but instead reinforces rigid conceptions of national identity. Here we may recall Stuart Hall's analysis of how a conception of diaspora, drawn from traditions of Jewish thought, nourished Black nationalism in the United States in the nineteenth and twentieth centuries:

> One reading of diaspora, after all, is precisely that linear story of the scattering of "a chosen people" from their natal, originary homeland; the preservation of their *ethnos*— their strong sense of cultural difference—in the face of all

adversity; how they held fast to their sacred texts; and how tradition was passed down through the lines of kinship and descent.[21]

The acts of upholding tradition, establishing genealogies, remembering the purity of an origin from which any deviation constitutes a degradation, believing in a promised land that one can return to even after centuries and historical conflicts as if it were one's due. Is it even possible to move away from such a rigid, conservative conception of diaspora? After all, if there are two narrative threads that cannot be pulled loose from the fabric of diaspora, they are continuity and filiation: one's loyalty to the supposed point of departure is affirmed, despite the distance. The diasporic map only registers one type of displacement that is free of spatial distortion: real physical distancing, and return (be it fictional or actual) to the point of departure.

~~Diaspora~~ Creole entanglements

Stuart Hall, Paul Gilroy, and Homi Bhabha have all proposed conceptions of diaspora stripped of its fundamentalist dimensions. For Hall, the term functions, in the space of the Black Atlantic, as a "metaphor" for the "discursive production of new interstitial spaces."[22] It is not so much a question of thinking about diaspora as it is about processes of "diasporization" in transcultural formations, born of the expansion of European empires starting in the seventeenth century, that produced spaces of cultural hybridization simultaneously developing relationships of hierarchy, violence, and power within. This process of diasporization could be likened to Édouard Glissant's concept of "creolization." And yet, the reflections of a thinker like Glissant are very thought-provoking here. In his work, the idea of creolization seems to be constructed in direct opposition to that of diaspora. This tension allows Glissant, initially, to cleave to Black memories of displacement and itinerancy. More significantly, it shapes his conception of the Atlantic slave trade as an absolute: the deportation of Black bodies from Africa to the Americas and movements of displacement or migration are incommensurable. Glissant thus rejects the idea of diaspora as a means to conceptualize new forms of globalities that unfold in the Caribbean and are born out of the abyss of the Atlantic slave trade:

> There is a difference between the transplanting (by exile or dispersion) of a people who continue to survive elsewhere and the transfer (by the slave trade) of a population to another place where they change into something different, a new set of possibilities.[23]

This short quotation from *Caribbean Discourse* interrogates the notion of diaspora as continuity, and more specifically, the spontaneous imposition of a meaningful relationship between the Caribbean archipelago and continental Africa. This substantial relationship between these spaces is at the heart of some Black nationalist writings informed by "back-to-Africa" teleologies (e.g., Marcus Garvey).[24] Glissant's position is clear: the history of the slave trade precludes any use of the notion of diaspora to conceive a unified Black world, emerging from an original referent, Africa. The ocean currents that carried the slave ships drowned the signifier *Africa* in deep ocean waters, delivered their human cargoes to naked violence, and ruptured genealogies and filiations. Whereas Saidiya Hartman writes that "for those chained in the lower decks of a slave ship, race was both a death sentence and the language of solidarity,"[25] Glissant is skeptical of any such solidarity. Tracing the routes of modern slavery, we observe the invention of a people that did not yet exist in the African territories they were forced to leave behind. We cannot therefore think of a diaspora, which implies a continuity, let alone apply those archaisms that would confine thought: "race," "nation," "roots," "genealogy," "territory." The Caribbean, for Glissant, is not a "Black world," and its people are not a "people in diaspora": it is a "new world fact," as he makes clear in the early pages of *Introduction to a Poetics of Diversity*:

> Whereas the Caribbean Sea is a sea that diffracts, and so leads us into the turmoil of diversity. It is not only a sea of transit and passage, but also of encounters and involvements. What has been happening in the Caribbean for the last three centuries is literally this: a coming together of cultural elements from absolutely diverse horizons, which become truly creolized, which really interlink and mix with one another to produce something absolutely unforeseeable, absolutely new: Creole reality.[26]

To conceptualize the Caribbean space we need new words, new images, and a poetics capable of doing justice to this radical creation, which opens our eyes to the reality of Glissant's *Tout-monde* ("whole-world"): an unprecedented co-presence, in a single place, of imaginaries, of beings and things, which certainly bears witness to asymmetries and histories of violence, but can in no way be apprehended through the language of territorial, racial, or cultural exclusivity. The term *creolization*, which describes the reality of Caribbean worlds born of the slave trade, rejects the conviction that "the identity of a being is only valid and recognizable if it excludes the identity of all other possible beings."[27] Creolization, then, describes the unpredictability of a generalized process of cultural hybridization in which the experience of the root appears neither central nor real.

The world born of the Atlantic slave trade established a linkage, between heterogeneous elements, that does not require racial signifiers or the continental referent *Africa* to be described and thought of as such. Thinking about creolization is not about conceiving a root, that is, a genealogy or continuity. Conceptualizing creolization means never thinking about a diaspora. By refusing to use the term *diaspora* to consider the genesis of Caribbean worlds that emerge out of the slave trade, Glissant examines the nature of a kind of violence that would be euphemized by suggesting that it was possible for something to maintain itself and gestured toward a solid, fixed origin in spite of its uprooting. If diasporic movement exists, it would have to be possible, even without physically returning, to focus on a point of departure located on a map.

But the violence of the transfer (*transbord* in Glissant's French evoking the shipment of people as freight) precludes the possibility of locating the coordinates of a terrestrial point of origin—the name of a village, family home, or linguistic region. For those that emerge out of the ship's hold, the only origin available is the ocean's gaping abyss. Both here and in the teleologies of return running through political imaginaries in Black Caribbean and American spaces throughout the nineteenth and twentieth centuries, Africa is no more than a topographical signifier that disguises the effectiveness of a negation—an impossible allegiance, an impossible filiation. So extreme was the violence that it foreclosed the very possibility of elaborating a valid poetic, political, and eschatological imaginary around the idea of a *promised land*. No land appears as a promise; no land is anyone's due.

By casting off the term *diaspora*, Glissant cleaves to Black memories: not all movements of Black bodies relate in the same way to planetary elements—continents, islands, archipelagos, seas, or oceans. More importantly, the creolization process, which describes Caribbean worlds that materialized from the slave trade, is itself undergoing globalization, bringing to light new terrain ushered in by the decline and fall of European empires beginning in the second half of the twentieth century. It is difficult to say with certainty that the term *diaspora* best encapsulates these cultural hybridizations. Diaspora, as an idea, seems to propose a single narrative framework: the drawing into tension of two territorial anchorages, on opposite ends, with a point of departure (real or imagined) on one side and a point of arrival and/or adopted home on the other.

Ubiquity and double presence

It is indeed this narrative framework of relation between two lands that is discursively explored when we attempt to chart a course using the idea of diaspora. For diaspora describes a terrestrial condition—that is, the way a subject inhabits *a given* land, by leaving it behind or settling in. How is it that, even after arriving in a land or country, and regardless of the circumstances of leaving, some continue to claim the land left behind or considered to be a birthright? Does engaging with such narrative require adhering to a rigid, substantive approach to cultural identity? How can we explain that certain lands, even though we no longer or have never lived in them, exert a lasting hold on us? Not as some desire for elsewhere, plucked from the air *in abstracto,* but rather as a physical anchor point in which a portion of our biography plays out while being constantly reinvented? All these questions run through the narrative framework of diasporic stories. They are anchoring narratives, narratives of conflicting terrain, resignified affectively, symbolically, or materially in the lives of subjects. These narratives establish relations from two identified spaces or territorialities and may offer a point of view on Glissant's *Tout-monde,* but they are *not* narratives of the *Tout-monde.* They are born of a terrestrial way of living where *at least* two spaces (a land of departure and a land of arrival) enter into relation with each other, to the exclusion of all others. By seeking to express a continuity that affirms itself against all odds—against exile, against displacement, against the radical nature of rupture—the idea of diaspora remains tied to notions of land and heritage (what has been passed down to us by those we are tied to and those who came before us). It can be mobilized, for economic and political reasons, by a state seeking to maintain connections with the members of a national community who live outside its territory. But it can also be invoked—and this is what interests me here—in the first person, in the indicative mood, by subjects re-signifying their mode of existence by claiming a second land in addition to the one they inhabit.

A subject can thus invoke their diasporic existence in defense of the possibility of *inheriting* a history inextricably linking them to one land even while they live in another, elsewhere. Defending the possibility of inheriting a memory of a place, as part of the very movement that de-territorializes it, has never meant preserving that memory as it is (as might perhaps be done by means of *pure memory*, preserving memories of the past whose essence, as Henri Bergson knew, consists in the impossibility of their being repeated).[28] Rather, it involves actively reiterating the memory: inventing it anew within fabricated forms created in a present that displaces it in order to extend its effects into the future, and perhaps other spaces as well. Far from a system of commemoration that ritualizes individual or collective memory, we are here engaging in a type of fabulation that conjures spaces of real, present, or past physical migrations that can define a subject's modes of political and cultural identification, along with their forms of belief, choices, or actions in everyday life.

When a subject claims a link, through its history, to a land it continues to inhabit while no longer being physically settled there, that is ubiquity. A double presence. Being and living in two places at once. A way of inhabiting the earth that ignores borders between the mind and matter. This ubiquity is an existential fabulation, charged with political potentialities. But it does not justify any inalienable right *to return*. Diasporic existences cannot be expressed in abstract terms. Each bears its own singular relationship to the land, to space, and to time, which requires a particular narrative—which could be a call to be reunited, the pressing demand for restitution after expropriation, or others still.

Let us return to the flesh from which this text is written, the people of Black France—French citizens or residents whose presence disturbs the national myth. Black France is a minority, not a unified body, and not a political subject. Any unity it may possess is strictly in the eye of majority beholders, outsiders, whose gaze freezes it in a mask of racial signifiers. Black France points toward the former island colonies of the Caribbean, the Pacific, and the Indian Ocean, and also toward the African mainland. This heterogeneity is overlain with memories which conflict from time to time. Memories of the ocean and the Atlantic slave trade are vessels conveying many relations to Africa that can be indifferent or painful, yearning or impossible. Memories of the African continent travel the routes of itinerancy laden with names, addresses, the exact coordinates of a family home, of a building or ruin, of ancestors and sometimes of relatives. The paths of these memories never cross. Their common denominator is not a continent. More often than not, it is a shared experience of contempt in which race weighs heavily on faces (turned to features) and on skin. The constant experience of racism, of its discourse, calls into question the conditions of a land's concrete habitability, when it unceasingly sends signs of rejection to the subject.

Claiming a second land affords an escape, at least in the mind—
something like a line of flight. Existing in diaspora enacts the
possibility, however slight, of remaining at a distance. It offers
a faint consolation: never condemned to a single land. Never
constrained to live there, even if we know, secretly, that the
other land we claim, which we may have fled under tragic circumstances, is not always a land of future promise.

The idea of diaspora does not pass over the brutality of
borders in silence; it demands of governments and border
agencies the right to a double presence—to live simultaneously on two territories that do not necessarily share physical
borders, to live in a given space over which another map super-
imposes its landmarks—locations, place names, abandoned
family homes or ruins. We must find a way to tell this; it is literally a marvelous thing. We must turn back to literature, now,
not as a last resort that will expose the weakness of refusing
to analyze diasporic existence in all its political, historical,
and administrative materiality. Instead of reasoning, we will
concretely show how such an *existing* can unfold, especially
on the border between a former Empire and its former colonies, where conflict is constant.

Nightmares and marvels

Life in diaspora unsettles clearly demarcated lines and
charted paths and re-politicizes ways of being—of living
and inhabiting—on soil that is constantly multiplying and
diffracting, and at other times cracks and gives way. It is not
a question of waiting for Glissant's *Tout-monde*, or of being

particularly sensitive to its rhythms, to the multiplicity of imaginaries and cultures that in any given place enter into relation with one another, but rather a question of detecting what, in each determined territory, reveals the dreamed or real presence of the other country we carry along with us and refuse to forget. Diasporic questions are always questions of anchoring, of an inscribing on the territory. Any reaffirmation of filiation is a struggle—sometimes joyful, sometimes desperate—against forgetting. It is for this reason alone that we use the term "diaspora." Literature possesses tools to give voice to this simultaneity, expressing the modes of this double presence that connects worlds in conflict: to narrate several lands, several memories, the way in which dreams and the materiality of multiple territories are combined, the dismantling of time when the dead remain an indistinct presence alongside the living. It can describe a double presence, a ubiquity—living in two places at once. It is a question of moving away from a sovereign, transparent subject, as the center of a linear narrative—for it is precisely through this distancing that the literary marvelous operates.

In the realm of the marvelous, the world is no longer organized according to the laws of shared perception; it is governed by the non-ordinary, which ceases to be an object of astonishment. In 1940, the surrealist writer Pierre Mabille released an anthology of fantastic literature, *Le Miroir du merveilleux* (translated in 1990 as the *Mirror of the Marvelous*), followed in 1946 by a brief treatise on the marvelous, *Le Merveilleux*. Departing from a poem by Aimé Césaire published in *Tropismes,* Mabille elaborates on his theme:

The marvelous expresses the need to surpass the limits placed on us, imposed by our structures . . . It aims to overcome the limits of space and time, seeks in fact to destroy these barriers, it is the struggle of freedom against all that would curtail, destroy, and disfigure it; it is tension, that is to say something different from regular and mechanical work: passionate and poetic tension.[29]

The marvelous, Pierre Mabille adds, "blazes above the masses at the hour of their revolt."[30]

The marvelous, to quote the literary critic Tzvetan Todorov, belongs to a class of narratives that admit the presence of the supernatural, in contrast with normal perceptions of reality,[31] based on the principle of identity. Diasporic existing, then, invokes the language of the marvelous to describe: the refusal to institute administrative borders between two territories as an effective physical limit; ubiquity or double presence; the recomposition of genealogies summoning the living and the dead to the same family banquet; the entanglement of temporalities in which lived, experienced time intermingles with stopped time (as an exile holds in their memory the date of their forced flight, and, after finding shelter, longs to return); the absence of caesura between matter and spirit (while on a real physical land, the country in one's dreams is not just nostalgia but living in spirit). In the diasporic existence, time and space are dislocated—past and present coexist; future merges with days past. What is lived and experienced takes its place in the register of the marvelous.

At the First International Congress of Black Writers and Artists, held at the Sorbonne in Paris in 1956, the writer

Jacques Stephen Alexis released a manifesto describing Haitian marvelous realism in the arts and literature. To defend the marvelous is to defend a "social realism," which means refusing to amputate from the real the "procession of the strange, the fantastic, of dreams, of half-light, of mystery . . ."[32] The marvelous, for Alexis, opens up into another, denser dimension that represents not a negation but a deepening of reality. Rooted in Haitian soil, his conception of realism clearly radicalizes Todorov's definition of the literary marvelous; it does not merely define a textual structure, a literary genre, but develops a metaphysics, a total vision of reality. The world obeys a dreamlike logic, sending reason twisting and spiraling. Normal perception is truncated; it is missing the dreamlike or nightmarish strata that trouble reality.

In the Caribbean and South America, literary currents of magical or marvelous realism, too often co-opted as literary marketing concepts,[33] propose an expanded vision of reality that neither strips it of consciousness nor flattens it with the hammer of verisimilitude. In these territories, what must be spoken and written concerns the unbelievable. The marvelous is necessary to grasp life on the margins of the plantation system—a murderous system. It is necessary to bring to light the unfolding of the subject in defiance of perilous racist fantasies that coerce and imprison the body. It is necessary to paint the possibility of revolution—how one might break the chains of a system of secular violence. Breaches. Escapes. Defying the machinery of death. Such is the purview of the marvelous: narrate life, in its insolence, and fly in the face of negation. Who still believes in fairy tales? In legends? In these narrative forms that develop a singular ecology where all elements—animate, material, immaterial—are protagonists of the story? The literary marvelous is not exclusive to the so-called literatures of the South—as if the refusal of a certain form of verisimilitude could only be the business of others who live outside the West. Nor is it particular to the artistic expressions of racial minorities making their way in the Global North. In the marvelous, the rule to follow is not the rule of verisimilitude; it is not a matter of cleaving to the facts of normal perception.

Dreamy, utopian figures predominate in the literary marvelous, writes Ernst Bloch in *The Principle of Hope*.[34] The marvelous offers a rerouting—not a wrong way, but another way—at the moment when our normal perception of the world becomes too self-assured and has drawn maps in places where the movement of bodies remains linear, carried by a unified subject who is believed to have a distinct and clear vision of its environment. The marvelous is just that: an action of rerouting reality in its three-dimensional form (comprising failures, misdirection, and defeats). But how can we reroute, going forward, perceptions of reality in France, a territory so certain of its history and its borders—and one which, in its truncated self-awareness, has forgotten that its past has not, for at least five centuries now, been exclusively European?

A country is never mere territorial expanse—no *res extensa* in Descartes's sense. For proponents of conservative, nationalist thinking, a country—a nation state—is never an expanse, let alone a government; it is a person, a soul possessed of a substantial and immutable identity. Yet for those living in diaspora, a country—the inhabited and/or habitable space—is never a substantive unit. It is rather an entanglement of spaces where administrative, physical, dreamlike, and imaginary borders confront each other; memories of itinerancy, sometimes peaceful, often violent, take the place of nightmare or promise.

Existing in diaspora, in a fracture defined by the history of colonization and post-colonial times, means building a country of one's own that exists in no atlas. This country lives with its own time, its own references, its own conflicting terrain. If literature plays a role in any of this—in these stories woven together by mobilizing maps with uncertain outlines—it does so because it can endow itself with an understanding of reality capable of expressing ubiquity, as something certain, and not as a miracle requiring illuminations or blindness, the annunciation of the good news or the preaching of the good word.

My description of diaspora and ubiquity is no literary manifesto, my intention not to impose prescriptions and rules governing ways of saying and writing the diasporic condition. The diaspora has no literature of its own, though it requires a poetics—a combination of words and languages capable of expressing the crossing of boundaries. Literature constantly exposes us to the dismantling of the principle of identity, opening an indefinite chain of contradictions that no one is bound to resolve: being in two places at once; replaying past times in the present; experiencing a splitting of the subject that is not always desperate (being torn), but sometimes joyous (scaling walls; uncovering layers and worlds; following one's double into other times and spaces, and more). Perhaps, after all, the marvelous is the general ontological regime of literature, and each genre, from realism to fantasy, gives us a perspective on it. But to illuminate the diasporic condition as a spatial entanglement, literature works as a mirror: it tells us that the marvelous connects easily with modes of existence in diaspora. As a happy coincidence, it allows us to discard (though they remain lurking nearby) the weighty themes of origin and authenticity, or incompleteness.

Diasporic life is an ongoing experience of rerouting. The word *reroute* is derived from the Old French *desruter*, whose meanings include "to disperse, to put to flight." Diasporic lives never hew to the expected routes: they remain in place while they dream of return, and while they yearn for the country they have left behind, they do not necessarily wish to live there again. This is not an inconsistency but a way of life, which recalls filiations, genealogies, and new departures, and refuses, once the land has been left, to consent to forget it.

Walking barefoot

In 1930s Brussels, a Congolese sailor named Thomas Mvuemba who has landed in Antwerp is travelling around Belgium. In the taverns, Brussels' Black gathering places, he listens to what people are saying. Years earlier, pan-African leader Paul Panda Farnana delivered speeches on Black consciousness in this capital of the Kingdom of Belgium. In a Europe still reeling from the Great War, he demanded recognition for the Congolese who had died for the continent. The unknown Congolese soldier deserved a grave on Belgian soil. On the land of the colonizers.

The sailor listens to the grumbling voices in the taverns, beer-soaked and drowsy. A thread is being pulled between

Flanders and Wallonia and the lands of Congo-Ruanda-Urundi. The sailor listens. He listens some more. Then he takes a boat through the Atlantic towards the Congolese coast. During the crossing, he calls out to the crew. He calls for an awakening of Black consciousness against white rule.

Matadi. Shipments of Belgian goods are being offloaded in the port. As the dockhands unload, the Force Publique, law enforcement agents in the Belgian Congo, take into custody the recalcitrant mind stepping off the ship. He has cursed the King, the colony, the whiteness of wounds and of faces, and the unjust chaos of the world. The sailor is deported to Kwilu province. Far from his family, who know nothing of his fate. Or rather, they will find out far too late. He is quarantined in Idiofa. A small town built on a village site to provide the church and the colonial administration with Indigenous labour.

No one ever knew where he was buried. But soon it became clear that he was dead. To mourn a loved one or a family member, one can wear an armband. One can shave one's head. Or one can walk barefoot. Thomas Mvuemba's brother walked barefoot for months to mourn the loss of his brother. He walked barefoot at home. He walked barefoot at work. Sometimes, he walked barefoot while wearing an elegant suit. Always shoeless. To walk barefoot means walking without making noise. That way, even amid the bustle of human activity, one can hear the voice of the departed who wishes to be heard. One may perceive the wake of their passage, the borders they invite you to cross.

Leopoldville: June 30, 1960. "Oh Table Ronde cha-cha ba gagner oh."[35] Independence Day. On this day of celebration, the dead are not forgotten—on the contrary, they are hard at work.[36] Each dance step opens a grave or vault, summons a spirit that has not known rest since the Belgians established their presence. On July 11, everything comes to a standstill. The first signs of collapse appear. In the heart of the now free and independent Congo, Katanga secedes and claims its own independence from the unified nation. A region of the newly sovereign country declares war with Belgian support. Destabilization in the region stops time once more. The books tell the same story, again and again: African independences are more formal than real most of the time. With each new story of defeat, a new history of dispersion begins.

In 1970s Brussels, Congolese Marxist-Leninist, Maoist, and Lumumbist students tune in to a local radio station every week. They are resisting the new neocolonial power. Most have been blacklisted. The new regime gathers the names of activists to be killed. Factors of national destabilization. Penniless students armed with degrees in social sciences and humanities. They cannot return home and are now settled in the lands of the former imperial power. Like an irony, like an admission: independence has borne no fruit; it is not fertile ground for the future. They will have to don the clothing of mourning again. Not make too much noise. Listen, again, to the voices—imperceptible—of the dead who refuse to consent to oblivion. And walk barefoot. The steps crossing manifold times and soils. The streets of Brussels. The streets of Kinshasa. A village in Kongo Central. Matadi. The stopped time of the celebration. Family reunions forever postponed. Parents growing old, departing, without ever knowing their descendants born in the land of exile. Life has made its way, in spite of everything, in spite of the dispersion, in the big and small cities of Europe—Brussels, Antwerp, Amiens, and Paris.

To live in diaspora is to collect stories, where several maps are superimposed. We ask the elders for these stories when their voices, still alive despite the exile, can tell them. Or we search for them in the often incomplete archives of itinerancy. It is a question of re-transcribing, on other soils, the active powers of filiation.

There is no diasporic life without history, without the dynamics of fabulation, where we pass down, from generation to generation, the stories of our ancestors who walked barefoot for many months. Crossing borders (existential, physical, metaphysical) where the living meets the dead. Crossing territories (real, administrative, dreamed) transfigured by new terrestrial projections—like the dream of any people who, after long subjugation, imagine themselves sovereign on an independent and prosperous land. The stories of exile travel and are reborn on other soils. They continue to flourish, creating countries and inhabitable places—where diasporas live. For diasporic lives, when we refuse to consider them as ambassadors or figures of national loyalty or betrayal, repopulate the world with wonderful fables.

I myself inhabit one of these fables. Crafted and collected along a border where the maps of France and the Democratic Republic of Congo become entangled. There were many deportees on Congolese soil during the Belgian colonial period. Then the shattered dreams of independence led to more new departures. The Congo is a diffracted land—where the soil, full of riches and mines, is also a sprawling tomb where corpses and hopes lie together. Some of the bodies were driven into exile during the thirty-year dictatorship and ended up in Europe, often in France or Belgium. In the diaspora, we pass on to each other, in the secrecy of families, stories of revenants. We cut our hair. We wear armbands. And we walk barefoot, waiting for a day of celebration. When the past returns, we drink with the living. And in our stubbornness, we never relinquish our claim to the place that remains impossible—the place of the future.

NADIA YALA KISUKIDI

When it comes to art and creation, the idea of
a common, shared perception is inconceivable.
The truth is always a question.

Invention, then, is our inheritance too.

RINALDO WALCOTT

Towards
Another Shape
of This World

RINALDO WALCOTT

Returning to Naples from a day trip to the Amalfi coast, I look away from the coastline and towards the open Mediterranean Sea, where I see a tall ship with full sails on the water. A strange feeling comes over me and I think that just beyond the ship, just where it looks like sky meets water, is where my people are. The feeling and what enters my consciousness stays with me the rest of the journey back to the mainland, although I say nothing to my travel companions. I am not one who is easily drawn into, or by, what others call the spiritual or the sacred, but what I felt and began to think that day was experienced bodily. I have been troubled by it ever since.

The sensation of that experience stayed with me, and I have recently assimilated it as a strange inheritance in body, mind, and thought. When I say inheritance, I mean the accumulated histories, sedimentations of terror, and the production of ideas that have come to constitute at least one iteration of Black life globally, and that I have internalized as a source of how I make sense of the world and move through the world. This inheritance can be, and often is, at odds with other kinds of Black inheritances, like the desire to belong to clearly discrete nations, and is always in deep opposition to white supremacist and Eurocentric versions of the world. It is the inheritance of feeling, which is something more than a feeling, as Kamau Brathwaite writes in *Middle Passages*:

> to be blown into fragments. your flesh
> like the islands that you loved
> like the seawall that you wished to heal[1]

The Middle Passage as one route—and root—extends into our present time, wherein the Mediterranean for Africans, and the Caribbean Sea and Pacific Ocean for Haitians, are its still-dreadful contemporary extensions. But we have also inherited the antiblackness that attends our movement around the globe. Indeed, antiblackness is one of the foundations of how we might think of the manner in which nation-states seek to manage contemporary Black movement. The fear that a Black swarm will engulf more wealthy and white nations, and ruin them, appears to animate many a policy of immigration. The coming "hordes" of Black people psychically underwrite international migration policy. Interestingly, it was not always this way, as the evidence of the history of the Middle Passage attests—but that was Black people being moved by others, and not moving of their own volition. In fact, we understand all forms of contemporary migration to have been inaugurated by the historic forced movement of Black people from Africa. Therefore, it is not too simple to state that movement (itineracy) for Black people, especially across borders, is a profound political act.

More than two decades ago, I wrote about jogging as a metaphor for thinking about Black movement across the

Canada–US border from the time before the Fugitive Slave Law of 1850 to the present. I used jogging as a way to get beyond the technology of the ship but to still reference the movement of Black people across land borders as caught up in the same histories, if not extensions of them that the movements by ship inaugurated. Running to the border as resistance, a potential freedom, offered another side to the struggle for Black emancipation. I had offered jogging as a related, companion metaphor to Paul Gilroy's ideas about sailing and ships.[2] Gilroy used the ship as an iconic reference of Black movement post-Columbus to the early modern period as an index for Black diasporic formation across the Atlantic region. Two decades later, the Afro-Indigenous artist Paulo Nazareth would initiate a visual philosophy of performance through walking across the Americas and Africa not simply as a way of reconnecting to the land or being of the land, but also as a practice that inaugurates a new mode of being, a new sociality. Nazareth's troubadour practice requires us to consider what reconciliation, reparations, and the future of life might be. These durational walk performances link in new ways not only histories but peoples, and reanimate what a life without borders might be. Writing of Nazareth's work, I have argued that he makes apparent the theft of Indigenous lands alongside the theft of Black flesh from land. In his visual philosophy of colonialism/slavery there is no AND; there is no conjunction in his practice.[3] The border, you see, is a conjunction. It demands a before and an after in its insistence that a line is being crossed, and therefore a new disposition is imminent. In Nazareth's durational walking practice, the border is a barrier and hindrance to forms of being together; it keeps in place a shape of the world that prohibits new imaginaries, new modes of being, new cognitive orientations. In short, the border can hold at bay species transformation and evolution. At the center of Brathwaite's and Nazareth's philosophy is the question: What kinds of beings are we?

In Nazareth's body, walking is a method that goes well beyond what we have termed reconnection. Nazareth has walked from Brazil up the spine of South America, into Central America, and on to North America. Similarly, he has walked the slave routes of southern Africa, especially across parts of South Africa and farther afield on the continent. The feet, *his* feet, planted in the soil of the Americas and Africa that Nazareth traverses, return us to a claim that is more profound than where people have come from and what lands they have laid claim too. In Nazareth's walk-as-philosophy, to plant feet in the soil is to reinsert and reassert our species as one organism among others on and in the earth. Nonetheless, we should not assume that Nazareth is engaged in some post-humanist project where he seeks to breach the human–animal divide. Instead, Nazareth's walk-as-philosophy undoes modernist assumptions of progress beyond the technology that is the body, while reasserting the body as the most important technology of our lives. Indeed, this walk-as-philosophy profoundly disrupts the idea that the species' greatest achievements are those that extend our bodies into other realms: the prosthesis of our technological fetishism is exposed as Nazareth treks across the Americas and Africa, encountering others and fostering new modes of sociality among the oppressed. Nazareth appears less interested in the repeated story of our oppression than in producing a new narrative of our survival, and of what lies at the core of that survival.

I feel the need to tarry with Nazareth and his method of the tidalectic, a concept inaugurated by Kamau Brathwaite to localize the dialectic in his environment. This is how Nazareth regains the past and fashions a future—and in his philosophy I sense, and am drawn to, a life not truncated by oppression but emboldened by it. It is this sense of feeling emboldened that I believe those we call migrants possess. By this I mean that the desire and need to move, regardless of the reason, is beyond the logic of the colonial. In this way, even the colonizers' movements have been conditioned by something bigger and more ancient than they can account for. It is a colonial delusion that movement can ultimately be controlled. Nazareth's walks-as-philosophy reconfigure the tidalectic as that which is both ancient and new, like the waves Brathwaite watched as he developed the idea, noticing how the pattern of what the wave took away and what it brought in was always new, and yet old.

Present migrations, and coming migrations produced in the vortex of climate catastrophe—which is to say produced in the context of the last five-hundred-plus years—makes thinking about borders more urgent. Indeed, thinkers like Nandita Sharma and Harsha Walia have already been pointing out how the politics of migration is continually changing, so that today migrants are positioned as unfairly seeking economic advantage by fleeing particular national and sovereign places to impinge on others' national spaces rather than following the resources in order to live lives.[4] The category "economic migrant" is often deployed to position migrants as unfairly seeking an advantage outside their national context and impinging on others unfairly and illegally. The nation, and the achievement of national dreams and independence or sovereignty, is now described as the most important element of autonomy, at a moment when borders have become one of the most important determinants of what kind of lives people might live, if they are to live lives at all. The nation-state and sovereignty are now offered as if they are a panacea for solving the unequal distribution of the world's wealth. When nation-states fail, when sovereignty collapses, it is not global forces then that are blamed or accounted for, but instead the national citizens of those nations are blamed as if nations are independent of each other and all the global forces that shape all of them. Thus, statements about nationality and sovereignty are deployed not for self-determining political purposes but rather as a means to hold people in place while using the idea of homeland as a container for prohibiting potential movement. Even the word *migrant* is, in my view, a compromising way to describe people's movement, obscuring the essence of that movement, as if it is not inherent to our species. Instead, people's movement today is broken into categories so that managing their access to resources can be done in relation to the racial and geographical maldistribution of those resources. Migration to the wealthy West, despite the still small number of people who attempt to move to the West, is an important barometer of this system, and a starting point for how we might rethink global distributive systems. People's global movement strikes at the heart of capitalist organization and its instituted artificial scarcity. We call these necessary movements—which stem from an impulse that might well be cellular—"migrations" and the people doing them "migrants," but let me propose that the term *migrant* is an assault on being. It is unpoetic assault. It is an assault because it is our species' drive to move, for both survival and transmutation.

My extended engagement with Nazareth's walk-as-philosophy is conditioned by the practical act of walking for migrants. Most migrants begin their move(ment) walking, before the automobile, ship, boat, or plane plays a role in further movement. We are by now familiar with the images of the small boats crossing the Mediterranean Sea packed with Africans, Syrians, and others seeking what we call refuge in Europe. I want, however, to turn our attention to some of the other borders that people cross by walking. Those Canada–US and US–Mexico borders animate Nazareth's philosophy and pinpoint the analog walk of the migrant crossing borders without nation-state sanction. Take, for example, the Roxham Road border crossing near the Quebec–New York border that has become a small flash point in Canadian politics. This crossing has been used by some Haitian migrants fleeing the USA and entering Canada to seek asylum, and has highlighted the problem in international law that those seeking asylum should make their claim when they arrive at their first safe border. In the case of these migrants crossing over into Canada, the first safe place is said to be the USA. Indeed, for Haitian migrants who legitimately believe the USA is not a safe place for them, crossing over into Canada and seeking asylum challenges the "first safe place" requirement. It is important to note that under the Trump administration, and continuing with the Biden administration, Haitians have been returned in large numbers to Haiti. Therefore, it is sensible that any Haitian seeking a safe harbor might attempt to go to Canada. Indeed, the Canadian government under the leadership of Prime Minister Justin Trudeau dispatched Creole-speaking representatives to Florida and New York to urge Haitian migrants not to make the trek to Roxham Road. People nonetheless continue to walk there, and to other less traveled US–Canada border crossings, to seek asylum.[5]

Migrants are not just moving from the USA to Canada but also the other way around. In early 2022 it was reported that an Indian family, the Patels, crossing into the USA froze to death while making the attempt.[6] The family reportedly died in temperatures of twenty below zero in the borderland between nations. The border crossing in question, between Manitoba and North Dakota, is one that "smugglers" use to move people into the USA who for one reason or other are not able to travel there through state-sanctioned movement. These family members died in a blizzard that made it impossible to see where they were going in what was difficult terrain on the best of days. Commentators have wondered why people take the risk of such crossings, and their inability to arrive at a satisfactory answer is, I think, embedded in Nazareth's walk philosophy. The four members of the Patel family—a son, a daughter, a mother, and a father—were seeking to be reunited with relatives in the USA and begin a new life there. A state-sanctioned means of international movement was not accorded to them in a timely manner, and thus they sought out what is referred to as illegal travel into the USA after "lawfully" entering Canada. This kind of multiple transit, partly "legal" and partly "unlawful," to reach a final destination highlights how borders contain people rather than facilitate their desired movement. But what is also uncontainable by borders is the affective and psychic desire of our species for encountering kin and others, and this occurs through movement.

Another example came in September 2021, when images circulated around the world of US border agents chasing, whipping, and pushing migrants while on horseback in Del Rio, Texas. Many of these migrants had walked the spine of South and Central America to reach the Mexico–US border. These are people similar to those Nazareth encounters on his own walks of that regional spine. The images recalled 1950s and 1960s Wild West movies, where men on horseback subjugated and punished Indigenous peoples, pushing them off their land as it was cleared for white colonial settlements. These images also remind us that the invisible lines that mark borders are clearly visible through the exercise of violence at those sites. The violence at the border, along with practices of subjugation, for some people even as there is unimpeded fluidity of movement for others (not all people encounter violence at the border) is what makes borders visible as terrains to be controlled and managed. What we witness in these whippings and frozen deaths, or in imprisonments in former Olympic stadiums and so on, is that the migrant is not headed towards some utopia but remains in the real world of adjudicated violence even when headed towards a life that promises to be different from the one left behind. Movement, then, is no guarantee of the absence of violence, even though it might decrease in intensity or be less targeted or present itself in a different manner. Nor is movement a guarantee of economic success or even survival, even if one's chances of survival might increase depending on where one lands. The desire to migrate subtends something more, something more primal, for our species' life, broadly construed.

Harsha Walia in her work has been keen to demonstrate the colonial capitalist management of the border. Walia demonstrates that when movement is broken into many different kinds of migrant identity, that movement is managed in relation to capitalist exploitation. Migrant labor is different from migrants moving because of conquest and displacement; and migrant displacement is different from the movement of illegal or undesirable peoples, those who move without state sanction and so on. The many names for migration—*labor*, *refugee*, *displaced*, *illegal*, and so on—are the ways in which the violence of the border is (dispensed), legitimated or not. The category in which a person is placed determines whether that person is open to violence or not. Walia's argument is powerful in its clarity that migration crises are a function of the nation-state, capitalism, and ongoing colonialism—and in particular, a function of Western policies made international, exercised and enforced at the site of numerous borders around the globe. The US–Mexico border and the Mediterranean Sea have emerged as the most iconic borders in our contemporary moment, insofar as they are the access points to global capital's excess. But as I suggested above, other borders make painfully clear what is at stake. Indeed, the ongoing collusive tensions between the UK and France concerning migrants traversing the English Channel are another case in point. There have been reports that both France and the UK have left migrants in small boats in the Channel to perish or be rescued at the last possible moment—again demonstrating the violence of the border.[7] Walia's work helps us to understand how this violence comes to be and, most importantly, what it keeps in place: white supremacist colonial capitalism.

The response to the ongoing challenge of managing borders is often to retrench nationalism as the means of curtailing non-state-managed movement. The assertion of citizenship as the central root of belonging has produced a heightened context of us and them, of who belongs and who does not, and this dualistic thinking is enforced by guarding borders, deciding who gets in and who stays out. Against these retrenched nationalisms Walia offers instead an expansive and "capacious global proletariat," and labor solidarities that struggle against the last, but nonetheless intensified, elements of colonial forms. Walia's argument leaves in place certain assumptions about political community that, I think, require further unpacking. I would argue that migrant movement challenges the nation-form itself, and therefore requires of us to think about this form anew. What does the nation really mean? And why desire it at all? And what is self-determination, land, settler, and Native—and what do they require of us?

Both Nandita Sharma and Mahmood Mamdani have brought intellectual pressure to bear on who is a settler and who is Native in their work.[8] Mamdani is interested in moving towards the postnational state and Sharma is interested in a decolonized commons. In different but related ways, both of these thinkers draw our attention to imagining beyond the nation-form so that we might live better together. At the heart of each of their arguments are concerns about natives, settlers, nations, citizens, and of course outsiders of one sort or another—usually marked as immigrants or migrants. At stake in understanding the task of undoing the nation-form and its attendant violence is seeing how history and power together reinforce forms of exclusion that are given to us if there is no way of ever exceeding them. It is indeed the struggle to work with the past, but not to be entirely bound by it, that prevents us from inventing the world anew, again. Both thinkers are concerned with what actual decolonization might look like. Sharma puts it this way: "Practicing a politics of postseparation—the refusal to confuse categories of rulers with the people placed within them—is an essential aspect of realizing a decolonization worthy of its name." Meanwhile, Mamdani, who still wants something like the state, writes: "Decolonizing the political through the recognition of a shared survivor identity does not require that we all pretend we are the same; far from it. It requires that our differences should define who benefits from the state and who is marginalized by it." I would add: it is the people who move who make these tensions particularly acute.

Because we have never come to terms with the historic forced migrations of Africans into the Americas, and furthermore with the migrations inaugurated by that first forced movement—which is the foundation of the world we currently live in, alongside the European enclosure of stolen Indigenous lands—our fictions about what it means to move are still located only in Europe's imaginary. Our inability to construct new modes of organization out of the dreadful, violently intertwined, entangled histories that have given rise to a global order in which some lives are valued more than others remains the failure of our moment. It is crucial to note that livability is intricately tied to the unequal distribution—and efforts to maintain that unequal distribution—of the earth's resources. This is a system founded in the earlier moment of European expansion (post-Columbus) and its multiple partitions of global life, a system that ranks who might live and who might die. Capitalism—that is, the white supremacist global organization of stolen wealth, the invention of artificial scarcity, and an instituted racial order of distribution, value, and deficit—now determines who lives, who dies, who moves, who stays put, and ultimately who is therefore worthy of life itself. This cruel arithmetic of European expansionist global value ranks some lives, as presently experienced, as not worthy of life at all. This deadly arithmetic of value was founded and invented in colonial transatlantic slavery's ordering of peoples, geographies, and a range of other modes of being, including racial and geographical hierarchies. The resulting practices, ideas, and institutions that flow from such ordering still structure our lives. In other words: the afterlife of slavery still orders how we experience the world.

The colonial histories and processes that gave rise to contemporary life in the West not only haunt our present, their histories are not yet behind us despite our best desires, fantasies, and claims to the contrary. Every act of our daily lives contains, embedded, the processes or the seeds of the violence of our collective colonial encounters and their aftermath. Most importantly, the ways in which those colonial histories continue to frame our relationships to a frequently asserted, but mythical and elusive, egalitarian and democratic West remain a significant barrier to actual change and potential transformation. In essence: the myth of democratic superiority holds at bay our potential to make a new world. Our social, political, and cultural attachment to what we might call the "good life" in the overdeveloped, wealthy West keeps us dependent on our historical relationship to the hierarchal practices of colonial ordering and management, practices that are the foundation of our social rules, regiments, and relations, and of our institutional structures, procedures, and rewards. Crucial to this ordering and management is the way in which colonial histories and their ongoing legacies are produced as knowledge in formal education and beyond, including all the institutions meant to both manage and give meaning to life, or to what it is to live. Furthermore, certain national discourses maintain the unequal distribution of resources by reinforcing these as inherent to certain geographies and demographics—in short, the wealthy, overdeveloped white West is assumed to have simply and naturally acquired its wealth and its "functioning" institutions almost magically, as if they were preordained.

Lisa Lowe in *The Intimacies of Four Continents* and Amitav Ghosh in *The Nutmeg's Curse* have demonstrated from different but congruent vantage points how a global system of unequally distributed resources has occurred, and how wealth accrued in the West, and also how the ideas that flowed from these processes remade the world in very particular ways. The stories they tell are not happy ones, but of violent entanglements that require us to think differently about the constitution of our current world. Lowe writes:

> This economy civilizes and develops freedom for "man" in modern Europe and North America, while relegating others to geographical and temporal spaces that are constituted as

backward, uncivilized, and unfree. Liberal forms of political economy, culture, government, and history propose a narrative of freedom overcoming enslavement that at once denies colonial slavery, erases the seizure of lands from native peoples, displaces migrations and connections across continents, and internalizes these processes in a national struggle of history and consciousness.

In Lowe's ideas we can see the seeds that might produce contemporary migrations. The modern economy, born of colonial adventure, is most productive in Europe and North America. So why would others not move in that direction, especially if the modern economy is also the site of living a life?

Ghosh, writing about the search for and discovery of nutmeg in the Banda Islands by European explorers—specifically the Dutch—and the colonial violence that ensued, as nutmeg became an important wealth-producing commodity, concludes:

> If we put aside the myth-making of modernity, in which humans are triumphantly free of material dependence on the planet, and acknowledge the reality of our ever-increasing servitude to the products of the Earth, then the story of the Bandanese no longer seems so distant from our present predicament. To the contrary, the continuities between the two are so pressing and powerful that it could even be said that the fate of the Banda Islands might be read as a template for the present, if only we knew how to tell that story.

The violent history of the search for nutmeg, which includes both the brutal oppression and massacres of Indigenous

Bandanese alongside the movement of subordinated labor to the islands to produce the spice, is a microcosm of the kinds of dreadful and hopeful conditions that the movement of peoples creates. It is part of a now well-established field of study of the economic history of commodities and how they have shaped our global social relations—including studies of sugar, tobacco, cotton, tea, and coffee. Of course, in the aftermath of Europe's violent global expansion, and the Industrial Revolution that was fueled by Europe's extractive practices, no other commodity became as important as oil—or, more broadly, fossil fuels. And, as we know, fossil fuels are now our species' great antagonist, the basis of climate change and climate catastrophe.

Fossil fuels have allowed the West to more fully exercise its global reach—through ownership of a commodity, and through international trade laws enforced with violence and other coercive methods developed in the formal colonial period of European expansion. In our present time we live in what the late geographer Neil Smith termed "overlapping colonialisms"—the old colonialism of invasion, war, land theft, and seizure of resources through death, occupation, and so on; and the new colonialism of financialized relations housed in the West (within its banks, stock exchanges, and other financial institutions and instruments) and enforced through trade agreements and supranational trade organizations with national and international rules that point in the advantageous direction of the West, along with incentives or punishments that keep extractive and accumulating practices firmly benefiting only the West. All these processes work in favor of the West, so that it continues to hold the power and authority to change global arrangements, and to keep its dominant and powerful position as the arbiter of what life is, what it should be, what it might be, and what it could become. In this way, older colonial practices have been transformed into coercive inclusions of various sorts. Chief among those "inclusions" are nationalisms and claims of sovereignties that suggest we all have a place where we naturally belong. Migration suggests we are in places where we do not, supposedly, naturally belong, and therefore migration has to be managed—or so the post-enlightenment logic goes.

But I suggest that migration only needs to be managed because of the wealthy, overdeveloped West's ongoing accumulation of the earth's resources, as if these are its sole prerogative to own. And climate catastrophe will only serve to highlight this further.

Climate change and climate unpredictability, and the migrations that flow from these, will have people moving to where the resources for living a life are being hoarded. They will be moving (and already are moving) towards the resources that have been extracted from their lands and turned into all manner of consumable and financialized products of our late-modern lives. At the heart of present and coming migrations lies a reckoning with global theft, the maldistribution of the earth's resources, and the violence that underpins it. As we assess Fortress Europe, with its multiple border mechanisms to keep others out; the apartheid seas of the Mediterranean, the Pacific, the Indian Ocean, and the Caribbean Sea; and the ever-increasing technological measures (drones and bio-metrics) that track and prohibit people's movement—including awarding them national "autonomy"—what we are really witnessing is the attempt to hold people in place and thus to maintain the unequal distribution of the world's wealth. And I suggest that climate unpredictability will make the desire to hold people in place even more acute.

As we face climate unpredictability, and as the impacts of climate change unfold, the idea and practice of the Euro-American West hoarding most of the world's resource wealth can no longer hold. To repeat: people will move—and by moving, they will make more explicit their intent to share in those resources. In 2021, the prime minister of Barbados, Mia Mottley, delivered a searing speech at COP26 that went viral for what appeared to be its truth-telling. Indeed, one of the seductive elements of PM Mottley's speech at COP26 was her insistence that resources were not being adequately distributed. She stated:

> On finance: we are $20 billion short of the $100 billion and this commitment, even then, might only be met in 2023. On adaptation: adaptation finance remains only at 25%, not the 50/50 split that was promised nor needed given the warming that is already taking place on this earth. Climate finance to frontline small island developing states declined by 25% in 2019. Failure to provide the critical finance, and that of loss and damage, is measured, my friends, on lives and livelihoods in our communities. This is immoral. And it is unjust.

The Barbadian PM's speech made clear who has the financial power to produce potential change. It is not, she stated, the small island states she was championing—the formerly colonized and new, emerging sovereign nation-states born in

the wake of Euro-American colonization and imperialism—
that hold the wealth to be distributed.

PM Mottley then followed up with:

The central banks of the wealthiest countries engaged in
$25 trillion of quantitative easing in the last 13 years. 25
trillion. Of that, $9 trillion was in the past 18 months—to
fight the pandemic. Had we used that $25 trillion to pur-
chase bonds to finance the energy transitions or the transition of how we eat or how we move ourselves in transport,
we would now, today, be reaching that 1.5°C limit that is so
vital to us.

I say to you today in Glasgow, that an annual increase
in the [Subsidy Dependence Indices] of $500 billion a year
for twenty years put in a trust to finance the transition is
the real gap, Secretary General, that we need to close. Not
the $50 billion being proposed for adaptation. And if $500
billion sounds big to you, guess what? It is just 2% of the
$25 trillion. This is the sword we need to wield.

I quote from Mottley's speech not because I agree with all
the details of her argument per se. Of course, her argument
does not sit outside a critique of capitalism, which, as I have
been arguing, is the foundation of the problem. I quote because
I think the argument has embedded in it the unspoken silence
of a claim too terrifying to make. The claim, the quiet part that
Mottley keeps quiet, is this: that the species moves, that this is
how we have evolved, that movement is central to who we are
as a species. At the root of her argument is the fear that the
people of small island states would be forced to move if climate

change cannot be interrupted. And Motley seems to imply that by providing small island states with the resources they need, these states would keep their peoples in their place (a kind of silent bribe). Put another way, the silent part of Mottley's speech is this: *Do you want the Black and other not-white poor masses showing up at your doors? Well then, invest in sustainable efforts.* The translation I offer here is the kind that cannot be made in supra-governmental meetings like COP26 because it would upend the massive infrastructures constructed to keep people in their place—especially people from the backward, made-poor Global South. The editors of the *Black Agenda Report* have made this very point about Mottley's well-celebrated speech:

> But it is also a depressing and quixotic statement on Black sovereignty when a country like Barbados—a country that is only just beginning to break the chains of colonialism— must beg for its life from the neocolonial powers. When pretty speeches are a substitute for direct action, while justice is invoked without plans for reparation, we can be damn sure those existential, ecological threats will be realized in the Caribbean, and everywhere Black people live. And they will not mourn us on the front line.[9]

We can see in these discussions that the old nation-state form has never been realized for many—and never will be, in a world under significant pressures to rethink our current mode of habitation. Indeed, what constitutes national sovereignty in the context of climate catastrophe will need urgent rethinking. Are we able to conceive of sharing the land without recourse to domination, conquest, and exclusion? The challenge that Nandita Sharma and Mahmood Mamdani offer us is much more urgent than it might appear: they ask us to conceive of living beyond the bounds bequeathed to us, those of European expansion's categories of life. This demand, and its insistence on ethical accounting of how we live together and partake of the earth's resources, is neither a forgetting of history nor ahistorical; rather, it asks us to invent new forms of human life, as Sylvia Wynter has phrased the possibility, of futures beyond Euro-America's political reign.

Our collective discourse on climate change has been largely silent about migration. And even when the issue is addressed, as we have seen, much remains unsaid. For example, the idea that climate-induced mass migrations are possible and could eventually change life as we now live it is often not discussed. What the prime minister of Barbados could not fully say at COP26 was that any major climate catastrophe in the region would surely result in mass movement, likely reaching all the way to North America. What also remains unsaid is that such mass movement would likely initiate new forms of human life, in that the movement would compel us to live differently together and to rethink post-enlightenment ideas of who belongs where, and why. Our continued silence on the profound impact of movement on our species' evolution is one element of the crisis in meaning that we are currently experiencing when we imagine what it means to live a life. How we make sense of what it means to live a life—what meaning we agree on collectively about what a life actually is—is entangled in an essential way with the crises of environment that we are in the early throes of experiencing, globally. The long five-hundred-plus years of Euro-American expansion and domination of the globe are now, more than ever, under significant stress of dissolution—and will surely dissolve as climate change demands that people move to ensure potential survival. Climate change might, in fact, be the impetus for the radical decolonization that many have worked for; and it may be our descent into full-on barbarity.

I can see only two options ahead of us.

The late eminent philosopher Stuart Hall, thinking critically about different phases of globalization, pointed out that, in the twenty-first century, "migration is the joker in the globalization pack." He continued,

> It intersects directly with the larger pattern of the North-South divide—the division between the overdeveloped "West" and the underdeveloped "rest" which contemporary globalization reproduces and underpins. In the new globalization, everything moves with a new fluidity: capital, investment, goods, messages, images. Only labor—people—are supposed to stay still. In this way, transnational corporations and world trade can take competitive advantage of spatialized inequalities.[10]

Hall continued: "Nevertheless, against the grain of the system, the second half of the 20th century and the first years of the 21st have seen an unprecedented explosion of largely unplanned movement of peoples." The coming migrations because of climate change will further confirm Hall's insight that "unplanned movement of peoples" will be a significant element of our present/future.

Furthermore, Hall's thinking helps us to imagine how new forms of creolization and hybridity, and therefore culture, can emerge from these migrations and produce new forms of community and social life. I extend Hall's insight to suggest that these migrations that soon will take place—or are now taking place—against the grain of white supremacist imperialist capitalism hold within them the seeds for our species' transformation beyond the current multiple hierarchies of colonial/slavery's expansionist Euro-American order. My argument is that it is in the unplanned migrations of the world's poorest, pushed by climate change, that the promise lies—the promise of new evolutionary forms of our species to invent new forms of political community.

This brings us firmly up against the crisis and struggle of, and for, meaning in our age of information. The politics and logics of reconciliation and reparations as we presently conceive of them remain too puny, too small, to animate new forms of life and new practices of sociality. Both reconciliation and reparations, as presently imagined, mostly keep the current shape of the world intact. Indeed, the demands of reconciliation and reparations are not new modes of thought, but rather extensions of the already deadly logics that make them appear legitimate in the first instance. To induce a new shape of this world requires new modes of thought. Édouard Glissant provides us with one way of conceptualizing what lies with us now, and ahead of us too: *chaos monde*. Glissant's chaotic society, or chaotic world, borders on anarchy, and it is this anarchy that gives us the possibility, not of escape, but of a route towards a new sociality. In Glissant's term, the possibility "is to imagine the unimaginable turbulence of Relation."[11] In my view, this "turbulence of Relation" means that we must risk the identity claims of the nation, of sovereignty, of capitalist niche difference, of the inheritance of European expansionist categorizations now called identity, that prohibit and imprison us in a terrible state of being, a state of being that I would argue is just before life. Such an acknowledgment does not bring us to a kumbaya moment, but places us in a confrontation with what Glissant calls the highest point of knowledge—a poetics.[12]

In Naomi Klein's *This Changes Everything: Capitalism vs. the Climate*, the author explicitly argues that capitalism is the problem that drives climate change and all the terrible consequences that stem from it. Klein is clear that a transition away from capitalist life is urgently needed if we are to collectively survive the species-induced climate catastrophe in which we are already living. Klein's critique of capitalism, and her assertion of our need to transition away from it, demands we recognize not only that climate change changes everything in light of its disaster, but that, as Ruth Wilson Gilmore argues concerning abolition and racial capitalism, we must change everything. Klein and Gilmore overlap, but with important and different emphases. To change everything that climate change has changed requires a new understanding of what constitutes political community, and a new understanding of the work we must do to make a political community beyond our dreadful late-modern inheritances.

To argue for a new form of political community is not to argue for the easy jettisoning of the history of structural relations, or ignoring the outcomes of a post-Euro-American expansionist world, or denial of the brutal, violent outcomes of that expansion. This is not an argument for historical forgetting, nor a color-blind world, nor a magical equality. It may well be impossible to put the unleashing of Europe's racially enforced hierarchies behind us, but those racial inventions—now made into forms of community and belonging, but also, importantly, into forms of division, as Sharma and Mamdani point out—do not have to remain the ruling norms of planetary life. Walia reminds us of what is long owed to those colonized and what would be necessary to repair and repay if planetary life is to be rebalanced. In such an articulation one can hear where we must begin our transformation—and we might also hear an urgent call for new imaginaries about how we might live better together. Such an understanding requires us to move beyond the kind of selves that we now inhabit through Euro-American categorizations. In short, we must reinvent both our relations and our poetics, which is to say: we must reinvent our language, and therefore our imaginations.

The languages we have now for the work we must do remain totally inadequate to the task of creating a new livability. What is the poetics of contemporary political organizing? Of political activism? Never in my life have I witnessed so many claiming to be organizers and activists, even as the conditions of global life speedily deteriorate. What do these languages, in their claims and rhetorics, conceal? What tactics are preempted? What strategies foreclosed? Who leads? And who follows? Who gets organized? It is at this juncture that the crisis of meaning reveals itself most profoundly, because our demands are not clear. And yet, still people move, and with their movement, new evolutionary possibilities reveal themselves—a revelation that is both conscious and unconscious. We might begin by imagining and naming the world we need, which means confronting, and expunging from our imaginaries, capitalism, nationalism, sovereignty as property, and modes of being that are seen to be inherent but, as we know, were ushered in by European expansion and super-exploitation. In fact, articulating a new architectonics of life—what Glissant calls poetics—is the task ahead of us if we want it to be so. Such a new architectonics of life would require us to rethink what we actually mean by life itself, what living is and might be, to rethink and even reexperience encounters and movement differently from how we currently experience them, and thus all the forces that make us who we think we are and, more importantly, who we might be. An entirely new philosophy of the species beyond what has animated our thought to date. To arrive at such a new imaginary, we will have to take risks. We will have to risk facing that the Euro-American hold on our imagination exists only because of its attendant violence. We will have to free our imaginations to conceive of new forms, configurations, and modalities of life and living; and we will have to risk articulating and uttering them as real, as actual. And in the meantime, what we can build as we move towards another shape of the world are durational forms of refusal and co-mingling, thereby evolving our political communities. These new architected communities of refusal, deliberately and consciously conceived as oppositional and future-oriented—these new communities of ethical care and political comity—can become the foundations for new forms of sociality. We should do more now than simply quote Fanon's leap of invention as the end of an anticolonial intervention and analysis; we might risk taking the leap to invent.

The new forms of sociality I am imagining will require our ongoing invention of new languages of the collective. We might begin with Ruth Wilson Gilmore's "small-c communism without the party," but we will also need to expand our present mode of knowledge.[13] This means risking rethinking—which is to say, risking reinventing what land means, and what claims to being on other people's lands mean, moving beyond Euro-American territory-izing categorial-izations of what and who a people are. In short, a new poetics of life demands a new account of land, an account that takes us *beyond* a response to European expansionist logics and their historic theft of lands everywhere. We can invent beyond diversity and all that flows from it, knowing that diversity is needed as an idea only because Euro-American dominance still orients our shared world. To stick with diversity as a marker of our multiplicities is to suggest we cannot surpass such dominance. It is to remain locked in a deadly embrace with white supremacy. We can and we must unlock that embrace. Invention, then, is our inheritance too. Our species' imperative to survive—another inheritance— might be our only common bond until a new shape of the world is made possible by the defeat of white supremacist Euro-American-centrism. The new shape of the world is the end of this one, and the unfolding of bodily sensation that only a freedom we have yet to know will allow us to discern and feel.

The sensation I felt on that trip along the Amalfi coast was not sacred to me, but it was a kind of call or alarm to reckon with the urgency of inventing a new fable of, and for, life— the call to be homonarans was bodily felt. Our intellectual orbit of meaning should exceed a response to Euro-American-centrism reaching to *chaos monde*. It should be a radical undoing, so that the new might emerge. My sentiments here might appear utopian to some, but I leave you with this thought: What might it mean to live a life, if we can't risk desiring and working towards utopia?

NOTES AND
REFERENCES

"Wey Dey Move"

DELE ADEYEMO

NOTES

1. Narrative quoted from National Museum of the American Indian, *Stellar Connections: Explorations in Cultural Astronomy—Pt. 4, Babatunde Lawal*, Video, 1:08:44, October 24, 2012, https://learninglab.si.edu/q/r/15416. With additional reference to Jacob Olupona, *City of 201 Gods: Ilé-Ifè in Time, Space, and the Imagination* (Berkeley, CA: University of California Press, 2011), 29.

2. Dionne Brand, *A Map to the Door of No Return* (Toronto, ON: Doubleday Canada, 2001), 18.

3. Olaudah Equiano, *The Interesting Narrative of the Life of Olaudah Equiano* (London, 1789).

4. Nathan Nunn, "The Long Term Effects of Africa's Slave Trades," *Quarterly Journal of Economics* 123 (2008): 139–176.

5. What's more, the demographic modeling of African populations undertaken by Manning (1990) and expanded on by Nunn (2008) shows that Africa's ability to form stable social and political institutions was significantly undermined by the dramatic depopulation that took place due to four slave trades in operation since the fifteenth century, principal amongst which was the transatlantic slave trade. As Nunn concludes, "a robust negative relationship exists between the number of slaves exported from each country and subsequent economic performance" (Ibid.).

6. Kristin Mann, *Slavery and the Birth of an African City* (Bloomington, IN: Indiana University Press, 2007); W. E. Burghardt Du Bois, "The Realities in Africa: European Profit or Negro Development?" *Foreign Affairs* 21 (1943): 721–732.

7. Frantz Fanon, *The Wretched of the Earth* (London: Penguin, 2001).

8. In my PhD, *Last Dark Continent* (forthcoming 2023), I argue that slavery is the ghost in the machine of logistics. I arrive at this formulation through: Christina Sharpe, *Monstrous Intimacies: Making Post-Slavery Subjects* (Durham, NC: Duke University Press, 2010), 27–29.

9. Brian Larkin, "The Politics and Poetics of Infrastructure," *Annual Review of Anthropology* 42, no. 1 (2013): 327–43, https://doi.org/10.1146/annurev-anthro-092412-155522.

10. Ibid.

11. Stephen Graham and Colin McFarlane, *Infrastructural Lives: Urban Infrastructure in Context* (London and New York: Routledge, 2014).

12. Saidiya V. Hartman and Frank B. Wilderson, "The Position of the Unthought," *Qui Parle* 13, no. 2 (2003): 183–201, www.jstor.org/stable/20686156.

13. Henry Louis Gates, Jr., *The Signifying Monkey: A Theory of Afro-American Literary Criticism* (Oxford, UK: Oxford University Press, 1988), 4.

14. Narrative quoted from National Museum, *Stellar Connections*. With additional reference to Olupona, *City of 201 Gods*, 29.

15. AutoReportNG, "See When Musa Yar'Adua Commissioned the Lagos–Ibadan Express Way (Throwback Video, Photos)," *AutoReportNG*, May 12, 2020, https://autoreportng.com/2020/05/musa-yaradua-commissioned-the-lagos-ibadan-express-way.html.

16. *Nation* (Lagos), "Julius Berger and Agony on Lagos–Ibadan Expressway," December 2, 2021, https://thenationonlineng.net/julius-berger-and-agony-on-lagos-ibadan-expressway/.

17. Rinaldo Walcott, "Middle Passage: In the Absence of Detail, Presenting and Representing a Historical Void," *Kronos* 44, no. 1 (2018), https://doi.org/10.17159/2309-9585/2018/v44a4;

Christina Sharpe, *In the Wake: On Blackness and Being* (Durham, NC: Duke University Press, 2016), 26.

18. Stefano Harney and Fred Moten, *The Undercommons: Fugitive Planning & Black Study* (Wivenhoe, UK: Minor Compositions, 2013), 93.

19. Tiffany Lethabo King, *The Black Shoals: Offshore Formations of Black and Native Studies* (Durham, NC, and London: Duke University Press, 2019), 123.

20. Harney and Moten, *Undercommons*, 93.

21. This specific research is yet to be published. For previous related work, see: Damilola D. Fagite, "Managing Smallpox Outbreak: Colonial Authorities and Medical Policies in Southwestern Nigeria, 1903–1960," *West Bohemian Historical Review* 2 (2022): 141–58.

22. Geoff Iyatse, "Osinbajo's Prescription and Painful History of Naira Devaluation," *Guardian* (Lagos), October 18, 2021, https://guardian.ng/business-services/osinbajos-prescription-and-painful-history-of-naira-devaluation/.

23. J.F. Ade Ajayi, Anthony Hamilton, Millard Kirk-Greene, Reuben Kenrick Udo, and Toyin O. Falola, "Economy of Nigeria," *Britannica*, July 26, 1999, www.britannica.com/place/Nigeria/Economy.

24. Mallam Mudi Yahaya, "Circadian Rhythms—The Many Layers of Lagos," in *Ten Cities: Clubbing in Nairobi, Cairo, Kyiv, Johannesburg, Berlin, Naples, Luanda, Lagos, Bristol, Lisbon, 1960–Present*, ed. Johannes Hossfeld Etyang and Joyce Nyairo (Leipzig, Germany: Spector Books, 2021).

25. Wole Soyinka, *The Open Sore of a Continent: A Personal Narrative of the Nigerian Crisis*, W.E.B. Du Bois Institute (Oxford, UK and New York: Oxford University Press, 1997), 80.

26. Ibid., 66.

27. Olupona, *City of 201 Gods*.

28. Stephen Adebanji Akintoye, *A History of the Yoruba People* (Dakar, Senegal: Amalion Publishing, 2010), 26.

29. Ibid., 29.

30. Ibid., 28–29.

31. Peter P. Ekeh, "Colonialism and the Two Publics in Africa: A Theoretical Statement," *Comparative Studies in Society and History* 17, no. 1 (1975): 91–112, www.jstor.org/stable/178372.

32. Wole Soyinka, *Death and the King's Horseman* (London: Methuen Drama, 1975).

33. Megan Vaughan, *Curing Their Ills: Colonial Power and African Illness* (Redwood City, CA: Stanford University Press, 1991); Wale Adebanwi, "Africa's 'Two Publics': Colonialism and Governmentality," *Theory, Culture & Society* 34, no. 4 (July 2017): 65–87, https://doi.org/10.1177/0263276416667197; Fagite, "Managing Smallpox Outbreak."

34. Jimoh Mufutau Oluwasegun, "The British Mosquito Eradication Campaign in Colonial Lagos, 1902–1950," *Canadian Journal of African Studies/Revue Canadienne des Études Africaines* 51, no. 2 (May 4, 2017): 217–36, https://doi.org/10.1080/00083968 .2017.1302808.

35. Robin Law, "Trade and Politics behind the Slave Coast: The Lagoon Traffic and the Rise of Lagos, 1500–1800," *Journal of African History* 24, no. 3 (1983): 321–48, www.jstor.org/stable /181898; Olatunji Ojo, "The Organization of the Atlantic Slave Trade in Yorubaland, ca.1777 to ca.1856," *International Journal of African Historical Studies* 41, no. 1 (2008): 77–100, www.jstor .org/stable/40282457.

36. Yahaya, "Circadian Rhythms."

37. Oludej talks, "OBA OF OWORONSHOKI WAS 52 WHEN HE GAINED ADMISSION INTO UNILAG," Facebook post, 2018.

38. Isaac Abimbade, "Why I Charge OWORONSHOKI Residents N1m Per Plot—Oba Of OWORONSHOKI, Oba BASHIRU OLORUNTOYIN SALIU," *City People Magazine* (blog), April 11, 2017, www.citypeopleonline.com/charge-oworonshoki -residents-n1m-per-plot-•oba-oworonshoki-oba-bashiru -oloruntoyin-saliu/.39; Ganiu (masquerade performer) and Morufu (lead masquerade), interview with the masquerades of Oworonshoki, interview by Dele Adeyemo, November 2021.

40. Amitav Ghosh, *The Great Derangement: Climate Change and the Unthinkable* (Chicago, IL: University of Chicago Press, 2016), 35–37.

41. Nehal El-Hadi, "Poetics, Politics, and Paradoxes of Sand," YouTube video, 2022.

42. Ben Mendelsohn, "Making the Urban Coast: A Geosocial Reading of Land, Sand, and Water in Lagos, Nigeria," *Comparative Studies of South Asia, Africa and the Middle East* 38, no. 3 (2018): 455–72, https://muse.jhu.edu/article/712671.

43. Anna Lowenhaupt Tsing, *The Mushroom at the End of the World: On the Possibility of Life in Capitalist Ruins*, reprint (Princeton, NJ: Princeton University Press, 2017), 63.

44. A. W. Lawrence, *Trade Castles & Forts of West Africa* (London: Jonathan Cape, 1963), 141.

45. Albert Van Dantzig, *Forts and Castles of Ghana*, 5th or later edition (Accra, Ghana: Sedco Publishing, 1999).

46. Kunle Akinsemoyin and Alan Vaughan-Richards, *Building Lagos*, 2nd ed. (Jersey: F & A Services, 1977), 4.

47. King, *Black Shoals*, 4.

48. AV [Adindu Victor], "Confession," produced by Tempoe, October 22, 2021, https://genius.com/Confession-av-lyrics.

49. King, *Black Shoals*, 4.

50. Alexander G. Weheliye, *Habeas Viscus: Racializing Assemblages, Biopolitics, and Black Feminist Theories of the Human* (Durham, NC: Duke University Press, 2014), 4.

51. Akinsola A. Akiwowo, *Ajobi and Ajogbe: Variations on the Theme of Sociation; an Inaugural Lecture Delivered at the University of Ife on Tuesday, 10 June, 1980*, Inaugural Lecture Series, vol. 46 (Ilé-Ifẹ̀, Nigeria: University of Ifẹ̀ Press, 1983).

52. Cedric J. Robinson, *Black Marxism: The Making of the Black Radical Tradition* (1983; repr., Chapel Hill: University of North Carolina Press, 2000), 167–71, http://site.ebrary.com/id/10351498; Fred Moten, *Black and Blur* (Durham, NC: Duke University Press, 2017).

53. Robin D.G. Kelley, *Freedom Dreams: The Black Radical Imagination*, 20th Anniversary ed. (Boston, MA: Beacon Press, 2022); Robin D.G. Kelley, "'We Are Not What We Seem': Rethinking Black Working-Class Opposition in the Jim Crow South," *Journal of American History* 80, no. 1 (June 1993): 75, https://doi.org/10.2307/2079698.

54. Tina Campt, "Frequencies of Care," lecture presented at the Serpentine Pavilion, London, 2022.

55. Julius S. Scott, *The Common Wind: Afro-American Currents in the Age of the Haitian Revolution* (London and New York: Verso Books, 2020).

56. Aderonke Adeola and Donna Etiebet, "The Understated Significance of Nigerian Market Women," *The Republic* (blog), October 30, 2019, https://republic.com.ng/october-november -2019/significance-of-nigerian-market-women/.

57. Ijoba Wayde, "Hardlife," produced by Master D Concept, August 29, 2022, www.masterdconcept.com.ng/ijoba-wayde-hardlife/.

58. Saidiya Hartman, *Wayward Lives, Beautiful Experiments* (New York: WW Norton, 2019), 18.

59. AbdouMaliq Simone, "People as Infrastructure: Intersecting Fragments in Johannesburg," *Public Culture* 16, no. 3 (September 1, 2004): 407–29, https://doi.org/10.1215/08992363-16-3-407; AbdouMaliq Simone, "Ritornello: 'People as Infrastructure,'" *Urban Geography* 42, no. 9 (October 21, 2021): 1341–48, https:// doi.org/10.1080/02723638.2021.1894397.

60. In this context in Nigerian, pidgin *dey* refers to "being."

61. AbdouMaliq Simone, *Improvised Lives: Rhythms of Endurance in an Urban South*, 1st ed. (Cambridge, UK: Polity, 2018).

62. Dele Adeyemo et al., "For the Refusal of Unpayable Debts: An Artists' Roundtable."

63. Stephanie Busari, Nima Elbagir, Gianluca Mezzofiore, Katie Polglase, and Barbara Arvanitidis, "Nigerian Judicial Panel Condemns 2020 Lekki Toll Gate Shooting as 'A Massacre,'" CNN, November 16, 2021, www.cnn.com/2021/11/15/africa /lekki-tollgate-judicial-panel-report-intl/index.html; Lagos Judicial Panel of Inquiry, *Report of the Lagos State Judicial Panel of Inquiry into SARS Abuses & Lekki Toll Gate Incident*, Ministry of Justice, November 14, 2021.

64. Ibid.

65. Reekado Banks, "Ozumba Mbadiwe," *OTR, Vol. 2*, Otherside Media Limited, 2021.

"Walking Barefoot"

NADIA YALA KISUKIDI

TRANSLATION BY PABLO STRAUSS

NOTES

1. Estelle-Sarah Bulle, "Une certaine parenté," *La Croix*, September 15, 2022, 28, www.la-croix.com/Debats/certaine-parente-2022 -09-15-1201233338.
2. François Azouvi, *Descartes et la France: Histoire d'une passion nationale* (Paris: Fayard, 2002), 9.
3. André Glucksmann, *Descartes, c'est la France* (Paris: Flammarion, 1987).
4. Ngũgĩ Wa Thiong'o, *Moving the Center: The Struggle for Cultural Freedoms* (London: James Currey, 1993).
5. Paul Gilroy, *Postcolonial Melancholia* (New York: Columbia University Press, 2005).
6. Stéphane Dufoix, *The Dispersion: A History of the Word Diaspora* (Leiden, Netherlands, and Boston, MA: Brill, 2017).
7. James Clifford, "Diasporas," *Cultural Anthropology* 9, no. 3 (1994): 302–38; Robin Cohen, *Global Diasporas: An Introduction*, trans. Amanda DeMarco (London: Routledge, 2008).
8. See Frédérique Aït-Touati, Alexandra Arènes, and Axelle Grégoire, *Terra Forma: A Book of Speculative Maps* (Cambridge, MA: MIT Press, 2022), which includes the phrase: "Just as Renaissance travelers set out to map the terra incognita of the New World, the mapmakers of Terra Forma have set out to discover the world that we think we know."
9. Ibid., 3.
10. Ibid., 10.
11. Ibid., 9.
12. Dufoix, *Dispersion*, 285.
13. Maurice Olender, *Race sans histoire* (Paris: Seuil, 2009).
14. For more information on the August 24, 2021, law, see: www.vie -publique.fr/loi/277621-loi-separatisme-respect-des-principes-de

-la-republique-24-aout-2021 (in French, last accessed February 15, 2023).

15. Stuart Hall, *The Fateful Triangle: Race, Ethnicity, Nation* (Cambridge, MA, and London: Harvard University Press, 2017).

16. This is why thinkers such as Richard Marienstras, Stuart Hall, and Paul Gilroy saw in the diaspora the cradle of subversive political utopias that dismantle the logic of national majorities. On this point, see: Richard Marienstras, *Être un peuple en diaspora* (Paris: Éditions Amsterdam, 2014); Paul Gilroy, *The Black Atlantic: Modernity and Double Consciousness* (Cambridge, MA: Harvard University Press, 1993); and Stuart Hall, *Identités et culture: Politique des cultural studies*, trans. Christophe Jaquet (Paris: Éditions Amsterdam, 2017).

17. See the National Front's program for the 2012 presidential election: www.vie-publique.fr/discours/184668-programme-de-mme -marine-le-pen-candidate-du-front-national-lelection (in French, last accessed February 12, 2023).

18. See the December 2019 report of the French development agency (Agence française de développement, or AFD), which ascribes specific development roles to African diasporas: www.afd.fr/fr /actualites/les-diasporas-africaines-un-partenaire-en-mouvement; for an analysis of the role of diasporas as a new player in the French political apparatus in Africa, see Elisa Domingues Dos Santos and Sina Schlimmer, "Nouveau sommet Afrique-France: la continuité masquée de la politique africaine d'Emmanuel Macron," in *L'Afrique en questions* 61 (October 27, 2021), www .ifri.org/fr/publications/editoriaux-de-lifri/lafrique-questions /nouveau-sommet-afrique-france-continuite-masquee; for the transcript of President Macron's comments on African diasporas in France at the Sommet Afrique-France (African-France Summit) held in October 2021 in Montpellier, see Mustapha Kessous, "'Notre diaspora est une chance': E. Macron rend hommage aux binationaux," *Le Monde Afrique*, October 9, 2021, www.lemonde. fr/politique/article/2021/10/09/notre-diaspora-est-une-chance -emmanuel-macron-rend-hommage-aux-binationaux_6097732_ 823448.html.

19. Yves Gounin, *La France en Afrique: Le combat des anciens et des modernes* (Paris: De Boeck, 2009).
20. See the transcript of Emmanuel Macron's speech (in French) here: www.elysee.fr/emmanuel-macron/2020/10/02/la-republique -en-actes-discours-du-president-de-la-republique-sur-le-theme -de-la-lutte-contre-les-separatismes (retrieved February 15, 2023). Our translation.
21. Hall, *Fateful Triangle*, 163.
22. Ibid., 164.
23. Édouard Glissant, "Reversion and Diversion," in *Caribbean Discourse: Selected Essays*, trans. J. Michael Dash (Charlottesville, VA: University of Virginia Press, 1996), 14.
24. See, for example: Marcus Garvey, "Speech Delivered at Madison Square Garden, NYC, USA, Sunday, March 16, 1924," in *The Philosophy and Opinions of Marcus Garvey*, ed. Amy Jacques Garvey (Dover, MA: Majority Press, 1986), 122.
25. Saidiya Hartman, *Lose Your Mother: A Journey along the Atlantic Slave Route* (New York: Farrar, Straus and Giroux, 2007), 6.
26. Édouard Glissant, "Creolizations in the Caribbean and the Americas," in *Introduction to a Poetics of Diversity*, trans. Celia Britton (Liverpool, UK: Liverpool University Press, 2020), 5.
27. Ibid., 6.
28. Henri Bergson, *Matière et mémoire* (Paris: Presses Universitaires de France, 2008), 88.
29. Pierre Mabille, *Le merveilleux* (1946; reis., Paris: Fata Morgana, 1992), 40. Our translation.
30. Ibid., 41.
31. Tzvetan Todorov, *Introduction à la littérature fantastique* (Paris: Seuil, 1970), 180.
32. Jacques Stephen Alexis, "Du réalisme merveilleux des Haïtiens," in *Le 1er Congrès International des écrivains et artistes noirs* (Paris: Présence africaine, 1956), 263.
33. Jean-Pierre Durix, "Le réalisme magique: genre à part entière ou 'auberge latino-américaine,'" in "Le réalisme merveilleux," special issue, *Itinéraires et contacts de cultures* 25 (Paris: L'harmattan, 1998), 9–18.

34. Ernst Bloch, *The Principle of Hope*, vol. 1, trans. Neville Plaice, Stephen Plaice, and Paul Knight (Cambridge, MA: MIT Press, 1995).
35. Excerpt from the lyrics of the Grand Kallé song "Indépendance Cha-cha."
36. I am referring to the title of the magnificent book by Vinciane Despret, *Les morts à l'œuvre* (Paris: Éditions La découverte, 2023).

"Towards Another Shape of This World"
RINALDO WALCOTT

NOTES

1. "How Europe Underdeveloped Africa," *Middle Passages* (New York: New Directions, 1993), 49.
2. *The Black Atlantic: Modernity and Double Consciousness* (Cambridge, MA: Harvard University Press, 1993); *Black Like Who: Writing Black Canada* (Toronto, ON: Insomniac Press, 1997).
3. *Paulo Nazareth's Visual Philosophy* (Toronto, ON: Power Plant, forthcoming).
4. *Home Rule: National Sovereignty and the Separation of Natives and Migrants* (Durham, NC: Duke University Press, 2020); *Border and Rule: Global Migration, Capitalism and the Rise of Racist Nationalism* (Halifax, NS: Fernwood Publishing, 2021).
5. Kate McKenna, "Montreal's Olympic Stadium Used to House Surge in Asylum Seekers Crossing from U.S.," CBC News, August 2, 2017, www.cbc.ca/news/canada/montreal/olympic-stadium-houses-asylum-seekers-1.4231808.
6. Hannah Ellis-Petersen, "'Mind-Blowing Tragedy': Deaths of Indian Family at US-Canada Border Put Visa Sales under Scrutiny," *Guardian*, February 6, 2022, www.theguardian.com/world/2022/feb/06/mind-blowing-tragedy-deaths-of-indian-family-at-us-canada-border-put-visa-sales-under-scrutiny; "Bodies of Indian Family Found Frozen near U.S.-Canada Border

Won't Be Flown Back Home," CBC News, January 28, 2022,
www.cbc.ca/news/canada/manitoba/family-found-frozen-us
-canada-border-manitoba-bodies-1.6332011; Canadian Press,
"2 Men Charged in India in Deaths of Family Found Frozen in
Manitoba near U.S. Border," CBC News, January 16, 2023,
www.cbc.ca/news/canada/manitoba/patel-family-freezing-deaths
-u-s-border-charges-1.6715656.

7. Diane Taylor, "UK Accused of Abandoning 38 People Adrift in
Channel," *Guardian*, January 19, 2023, www.theguardian.com
/uk-news/2023/jan/19/uk-accused-of-abandoning-38-people
-adrift-in-channel; Diane Taylor, "UK and French Coastguards
'Passed Buck' as 27 People Drowned in Channel," *Guardian*,
November 12, 2022, www.theguardian.com/uk-news/2022/nov
/12/uk-french-coastguards-passed-buck-people-drowned-channel.

8. Mahmood Mamdani, *Neither Settler nor Native: The Making
and Unmaking of Permanent Minorities* (Cambridge, MA:
Harvard University Press, 2020).

9. Editors, "Transcript: 'Will They Mourn Us on the Front Line?'
Mia Mottley, PM of Barbados, Speech at the Opening of the
World Leaders Summit of the United Nations Climate Change
Conference (COP26), November 1, 2021," *Black Agenda Report*,
November 3, 2021, www.blackagendareport.com/transcript-will
-they-mourn-us-front-line-mia-mottley-pm-barbados-speech
-opening-world-leaders.

10. Stuart Hall, "Creolization, Diaspora, and Hybridity in the
Context of Globalization," in *Créolité and Creolization:
Documenta 11_Platform3*, ed. Okwui Enwezor et al. (Kassel,
Germany: Hatje Cantz, 2003), 185–98.

11. *Poetics of Relation* (Ann Arbor, MI: University of Michigan
Press, 1997), 138.

12. Ibid., 140.

13. "Abolition on Stolen Land" (Sawyer Seminar on Sanctuary Spaces:
Reworlding Humanism, presented by the UCLA Luskin Institute
on Inequality and Democracy, Los Angeles, October 9, 2020).

ABOUT THE ALCHEMISTS

DELE ADEYEMO (UK/Nigeria) is an architect, artist, and critical urban theorist. Dele's creative practice, research, and pedagogy interrogate the underlying racial drivers in the production of space. Adeyemo is completing his PhD, titled *Last Dark Continent*, at the Centre for Research Architecture at Goldsmiths, University of London. He is the recipient of the *Journal of Architectural Education*'s inaugural Fellowship, the Canadian Centre for Architecture's Andrew Mellon Fellowship, and Het Nieuwe Instituut's Research Fellowship. Adeyemo's projects have been presented internationally, including at the 13th Venice Architecture Biennale, the 5th Istanbul Design Biennial, the 13th São Paulo Architecture Biennial, and the 2nd Edition of the Lagos Biennial. He currently teaches an architecture design studio at the Royal College of Art, London.

NATALIE DIAZ (US/Mojave/Akimel O'otham) was born and raised in the Fort Mojave Indian Village in Needles, California, on the banks of the Colorado River. She is Mojave and an enrolled member of the Gila River Indian Tribe. She is the author of *When My Brother Was an Aztec*, winner of the American Book Award; Diaz's second collection, *Postcolonial Love Poem*, was published by Graywolf Press in 2020 and won a Pulitzer Prize. She is a MacArthur Foundation Fellow, a Lannan Literary Fellow, and a Native Arts Council Foundation Artist Fellow. She is an alumni of the United States Artists Ford Fellowship and now serves on the board of trustees. She is currently a Mellon Foundation Fellow. Diaz teaches at the Arizona State University Creative Writing MFA program where she is the Maxine and Jonathan Marshall Chair of Modern and Contemporary Poetry and directs the Center for Imagination in the Borderlands.

NADIA YALA KISUKIDI (France) is Associate Professor in philosophy at Paris 8 Vincennes–Saint-Denis University. She was Vice President of the Collège International de Philosophie (2014–2016). Member of the *Les Cahiers d'études africaines* (CNRS, Ehess) editorial committee, she was co-curator of the Yango II Biennale, Kinshasa, DRC (July/August 2022). Kisukidi is specialized in French and Africana philosophy. She has published *Bergson ou l'humanité créatrice* (CNRS, 2013), and *Dialogue Transatlantique* with the Brazilian philosopher Djamila Ribeiro (Anacaona, 2021). Her first novel, *La Dissociation*, was published by Seuil in 2022.

RINALDO WALCOTT (Canada) is Professor and Chair of Africana and American Studies at the University at Buffalo. His teaching and research are in the area of Black diaspora cultural studies and postcolonial studies with an emphasis on questions of sexuality and gender. He is the author most recently of *On Property* (Biblioasis, 2021) and *The Long Emancipation: Moving Toward Black Freedom* (Duke University Press, 2021).

CHRISTINA SHARPE is a writer, Professor, and Canada Research Chair in Black Studies in the Humanities at York University in Toronto. She is also a Senior Research Associate at the Centre for the Study of Race, Gender & Class (RGC) at the University of Johannesburg and a Matakyev Research Fellow at the Center for Imagination in the Borderlands at the Arizona State University. She is the author of *In the Wake: On Blackness and Being* (Duke University Press, 2016)—named by the *Guardian* and the *Walrus* as one of the best books of 2016 and a nonfiction finalist for the Hurston/Wright Legacy Award—and *Monstrous Intimacies: Making Post-Slavery Subjects* (Duke University Press, 2010), as well as *Ordinary Notes* (Knopf Canada, 2023).

ACKNOWLEDGEMENTS

Lectures series editor Christina Sharpe and Alchemy Books Editorial Director Dionne Brand wish to thank Marcelle-Anne Fletcher for her close and helpful reading of the translated text in Nadia Yala Kisukidi's lecture. Thanks to Penguin Random House Canada/Knopf Canada, including CEO Kristin Cochrane, whose enthusiastic response to this initiative has made the publication process possible; Adrienne Tang for her attention to international rights; Jennifer Griffiths for her striking design of the cover and interior, alongside Susan Burns and Christie Hanson for their care with the physical production of the book; Ashley Dunn for her marketing vision for the series; and the small, passionate Alchemy Books team for their care in shepherding the book through all its stages: Martha Kanya-Forstner, Publisher of Knopf Canada; Lynn Henry, Publishing Director of Alchemy Books; Hilary Lo, Editorial Assistant at Knopf Canada and Alchemy Books; and Genevieve Francois, our wonderful first Alchemy intern.

Above all, we wish to thank again the Lecturers for their leaps of faith, for agreeing to be the first, and for all the extraordinary ways in which they thought together, on stage and in the pages of this book.